Straightforward Publishing

Brighton BN2 4EG

British Cataloguing in Publication data. A catalogue record is
available for this book from the British Library.

ISBN 1903909 87 2

Printed in the United Kingdom by Webspeed Books Beds

www.webspeedbooks.com

Cover Design by Straightforward Graphics

Note:

This book is not intended for therapeutic or diagnostic purposes.
Further, the opinions expressed within are the authors.

Contents

Diagrams

DIAGRAMS

Introduction

For new readers, this book is neither narrative nor 'self help' but a broad ranging guide in plain language for the general reader. It may interest those with mental health problems, carers, new professionals or enlightened people who wish to inform themselves about mental illness; it's causes, course and recovery.

Not everyone will categorise anxiety and depression as mental illnesses but I am doing this for a reason; to reduce stigma by broadening the meaning of mental illness. When something is commonly accepted it no longer bears stigma. That is my belief.

Within these pages you'll find a whole range of illnesses of the mind described, from anxiety to schizophrenia; and a galaxy of treatments from electric eels to electro-convulsive therapy. No, I am not joking - read the chapter on historic treatments!

This book is my work of many years study, personal research and practical experience of working with clients/patients. It also contains the fruits of my personal experience of mental illness.

Stigma around mental illness is common. Patients and mental health charities are starting to dispel common urban myths but many people still cannot accept those are perceived as 'different'. They remain afraid of what they cannot understand. I have certainly found more tolerance, kindness and compassion among those diagnosed with mental illness than among many of the so-called 'normal' people I have had as neighbours over the last 4 decades. Great life challenge often breeds large souls.

Readers of this book will come to understand, that anyone can become mentally ill given the right conditions. And, as to public paranoia over schizophrenia; there is far more chance of a so called 'normal' citizen committing the murder.

I hope my book will help redress some of the stigma. As always constructive comment, notice of errors or new topic ideas are welcome.

I now wish to make a stand about the NHS, an institution I am increasingly dubious about. This is after all the setting to which mental illness is bound.

The NHS is undergoing a cash crisis which might take it to the edge of extinction. Do not waste your tears on this, because ultimately I believe this demise might prove to the good.

I am saddened to write, that there is ample evidence of increasing numbers of hard pressed clinicians being bullied at work. A union representative said to me that this behaviour was to be expected in the current stressful economic climate. I do not believe this to be true. It is certainly a poor excuse. However, it is indicative of the danger of putting both budgets and power over clinical staff into the hands of ill trained individuals with the wrong kind of personality.

What if there was a new order, of local services presided over by management consortiums of clinicians and service users who live and work in the area and therefore have a vested interest in providing the best of what is available, and at less waste and cost.

These teams could be lead by a tribunal of facilitators, trained in the crafts of leadership and logistics. This would obviate the current system of individual autocrats who hold both purse strings and power over staff; a system in which it is too easy to abuse vulnerable staff afraid of losing their jobs.

The hopes I had for a new order when I undertook my new degree in Mental health are dampened, not only by the situation I have described as above, but by the axing of this vital training for new staff in the values which underpin the treatment of those with mental illness; a training which would have improved careers, reduced inter-professional rivalry and brought forward a new age of managers versed in the art of leadership. Sadly, this is not to be; at least in the near future.

It is in the rather sad climate that I present this edition of **'Understanding Mental Illness'**.

Rather than write about the NHS in its current state I have, at the last minute, deleted this section from my book. I cannot support that which is corrupt, and I believe this is so because of evidence from many sources. When things improve, and I can honestly see a way forward that looks brighter and more hopeful, then I will consider a re-write.

I hope you enjoy this book. I have certainly enjoyed writing it. It is my heartfelt wish that the future will be brighter for all of us with mental health problems; I mean to say, everyone because no one is never touched by that state which Kay Jamison calls 'an unquiet mind'.

We all deserve peace of mind, in caring communities and a chance to grow our own special talents, to fulfil what we are capable of becoming as human beings. To live freely on this lovely planet we have been gifted.

Marianne Richards

Dedications

My brother

R.I.P. my friend and mentor Sylvia – I miss you

R.I.P. Betty & Gloria – I enjoyed sharing poetry with you

****

And in memory of all the people throughout history
Who have suffered greatly through mental illness,
because treatments were not available -
in the hope that their terrible suffering was not in vain.

'suicidal woman with melancholia and fear'
1892 lithograph
Wellcome Trust Medical Photographic Library

Tho' much is taken, much abides; and tho'

We are not now that strength which in old days

Moved earth and heaven, that which we are, we are--

One equal temper of heroic hearts

Made weak by time and fate, but strong in will

To strive, to seek, to find, and not to yield.

From Ulysses

by Alfred Lord Tennyson

Every night and every morn

Some to misery are born,

Every morn and every night

Some are born to sweet delight

Some are born to sweet delight

Some are born to endless night.

From The Auguries of Innocence

William Blake

Acknowledgements

I would like to thank the following people for their generous assistance in the writing of this book.

The Librarians and Assistants of Westbury Library, Wiltshire for unflagging help in obtaining the most obscure of books. Dr Peter Ager [longstanding GP, now retired], Dr Kate Kerr [Psychiatrist], Marie Anderson [Counsellor] for reviews of editions 1 and 2. Dr Ernest Gralton [Consultant Psychiatrist] for review of current edition. Ian for sharing his experiences of manic depressive psychosis. Gina, Sarah Joy and Sarah for excellent tutoring and much encouragement. Helena for much needed green teas and words of kindness. And finally Miss Proom; the student teacher who introduced me to the delights of classical music and poetry at the tender age of 10 and which have been major solaces ever since.

Copyright Permissions

Text
Crown copyright material is reproduced with the permission of the Controller of HMSO and the Queen's Printer for Scotland. Websites for the information on the Mental Health Bill 2004 are stated at the end of the chapter. Statistics reproduced on license from the National Statistics website: www.statistics.gov.uk

Summary of Mind proposals for the new Mental Health Bill kindly written & approved by Mind.

Images
I-stock Images [where indicated] - on license [permission of members of istock community stock photography] library. Suicidal woman with melancholia and fear (1892 lithograph) - permission of the Wellcome Trust Medical Photographic Library.

1950's ECT machine and electrodes & Neolithic trepanned skull - permission of the Science Museum

History of Mental Illness

"There is no health without mental health"
World Health Organisation

Chapter 1

Electric Eels to Antidepressants:

A Brief History of 'Madness' & Medicine

Contents of this Chapter:

Devils & Demons - Primitive Beliefs
- Revenge Of The Gods - The Ancients
- Greeks and Egyptians - sleep temples
- Evil Unleashed - Medieval Witches And The Devil

Social Degenerates & Misfits- The Victorian View
- Treatment in Asylums
- Early Psychiatry
- The York Retreat 1796
- Victorian Asylums

1970's - Hospitals - the New Asylums
Psychosurgery
- Phineas Gage - The Rise of Psycho-surgery
- Lobotomy

In Brief - Talking and Psychological Therapies
ECT and Drug Therapy
Anti Psychiatric Movement Of 60's And 70's
Closure of Asylums & Rise of Psychiatric Hospitals
A Broader Perspective for Treatment
- Move Towards Community-Based Care
- Virtual Brains - computer simulation

[The Myth of Oedipus Rex]
[The Myth of the House of Agamemnon]

When something is mentally wrong with a fellow human being, it is generally apparent they are not in a 'normal' state. The same would have applied throughout history, whether or not the people had an explanation for these changes. Throughout time, these explanations have been very different; evil spirits, acts of the gods, social degeneracy, immorality, or some inner cause.

For several centuries the term 'madness' has been in vogue. But what exactly is 'madness' and how does it differ from 'mental illness'? There are many derogatory terms; crazy, looney, psycho, schizo, mad[wo]man, maniac, nutter, loopy.. but these neither enlighten nor are meaningful. So, to start on this journey towards understanding mental illness, I thought I would start with a brief history of madness, the lowlights and highlights of beliefs and treatments. Treatment, as you will begin to learn, is closely connected with the way 'madness' is perceived by the community.

Devils & Demons - Primitive Beliefs

It is generally accepted that primitive people drew pictures on cave walls not just to decorate their homes or celebrate kills but as an act of faith. They believed that painting animals shot with spears would ensure successful hunts. This linking of imagined events to real ones was a vast intellectual leap; one of the features which separated mankind from their animal past.

This primitive magic extended into beliefs about the strange behaviours which we now know to be symptoms of mental illness. 40,000 years ago primitive people believed that malicious spirits and demons were able to enter through the head. Many 'trepanned' human skulls have been found from Neolithic times; these are among the earliest examples of a type of psycho-surgery. Trepanning was the process of cutting a circular hole in the skull to allow evil spirits to leave. Archaeologists noticed bone growth around such holes in primitive skulls which indicate that, astonishingly, many people survived this crude surgery. This practice was widespread from the Stone Age right up to 5th century BC Ancient Greece and was also practised by many other cultures including North American Indians. So here is an instance where community belief leads to a specific treatment being given to patients. Be reassured, that although psychosurgery [brain surgery] is still performed it is not for these reasons and not in the same way - with crude axes...

15

Neolithic Trepanned Skull

Trepanning began as early as the Neolithic age. It is thought that primitive people performed this as an act of powerful magic, possibly believing that evil spirits could escape the afflicted person via the head.

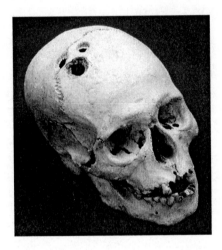

So, let's go a bit further forward in time. The Greeks and Romans were a bit more 'modern' in their thinking.

Revenge of the Gods - The Ancients

The Greeks recognised that continuous mental conflict [moral dilemmas] resulted in loss of sanity, a theory developed centuries later by Sigmund Freud. The Greeks thought conflicts were sent by the gods as punishment to arrogant men. In Greek tragedies the dramatic role of The Chorus (a group of masked actors) was to represent in spoken verse the moral dilemmas of the hero as he worked his way through his fate to his final [usually tragic] end. Two examples are the myths of Oedipus Rex and Agamemnon which I have summarised at the end of the chapter for you.

A highly regarded Greek philosopher called Hippocrates, who is accredited as the father of modern medicine, made a study of illnesses of the mind. Two thousand years ahead of his time he concluded that madness was "*no more divine nor sacred than other diseases, but has a natural cause.*" Hippocrates categorised three mental disorders; brain fever, mania and melancholia. He believed that four humours (or vital fluids) existed in the body and an imbalance of these fluids caused illnesses of mind and body. For example, an excess of black bile [one of the humours] was believed to cause melancholia; what we now call depressive illness.

Humours were balanced by bloodletting or purging a therapy which persisted until the 16th century AD. There is a parallel to the current medical model where psychiatrists believe that mental illnesses like depression are caused by chemical imbalances in the brain.

Plato (another Greek philosopher) said that madmen (his term) ought to be locked away at home by their families, a practice widespread in early nineteenth century England before the advent of Asylums.

Greeks and Egyptians - sleep temples

The Romans were familiar with depressive illness and tolerant of strange behaviours. They used what modern medicine would recognise as beneficial treatments; warm baths, music, well lighted rooms. Both the Greeks and Romans had sleep temples where soporific herbs were given to patients who rested and slept as part of their cure. Again, a form of sleep treatment induced by drugs was used until fairly recent times. It was called modified narcosis and given in cases where a patient was not responding to treatment and was exhausted.

The Romans reportedly used electric eels to administer shock s to patients, a practice used in Bethlem Hospital until the nineteenth century and curiously enough a precursor of electric shock treatment (ECT) which is still used (although under very strict guidelines; refer to the section on medical treatments). No one knows how this treatment works but it does seem to, in some extreme cases.

Evil Unleashed - Medieval Witches and The Devil

By medieval times sick people and animals were thought possessed with evil spirits as a result of curses put upon them by witches, the human servants of the devil. The Church, concerned at immoral sexual activity between its monks and nuns, blamed the Devil for inciting women to passion. So witch-hunts began, a terrible period of history when tens of thousands of innocent women and men were burned to death by the notorious Spanish Inquisition of the Roman Catholic Church. The book 'The Devils of Loudun' by Aldous Huxley graphically illustrates the story of one such victim. Again, we see the results of the community's beliefs having a marked effect on the treatment of mental illness.

Social Degenerates & Misfits- The Victorian View

In 1377 Bethlem Hospital became the first Asylum, funded by public subscription. Founded on the site of an earlier Priory (St

Mary of Bethlehem) it was originally designed to lock up people considered insane. In 1403 inhabitants included both physically and mentally ill patients.

By the sixteenth century monasteries and nunneries were enlightened enough to provide shelter for the insane within local communities. Madness continued to be regarded as an evil inflicted by the Devil which could be cured by prayer and bible reading. Asylum originally meant place of refuge. In effect asylums became dumping grounds for socially unacceptable people of the day; unwanted relatives, beggars or prostitutes.

Private madhouses existed in Victorian times and were run as businesses. Wealthy patients paid for their keep whereas the parish paid for the accommodation of poor people. It was common for people to be prosecuted and imprisoned for bizarre or anti-social behaviour. This crimilization of mental illness is a syndrome repeated in modern times. Criminal courts have to decide if serial killers for example are 'mad or bad'. As a brief aside, far more people who are so-called sane [mentally responsible for their crimes] are convicted for murder than so-called criminally insane people.

Although mental illness was not regarded as treatable in the same way as physical illness it was recognised that something had to be done about mentally ill people. When Bethlem was built none of the inmates were expected to recover. Most patients would die within its walls having been deserted by friends, family and their community.

Treatment in Asylums

Male and female patients were kept in appalling conditions; naked, often restrained or chained, with straw bedding. On Sundays the public were allowed to pay to view them for entertainment whereas serious visitors were discouraged. This was common practice until 1770 when it was banned.

Treatment consisted of vomiting and purging to weaken patients as this was thought to lessen the possibility of violence. It was considered wasteful to give patients too much food in view of this so virtual starvation was common. Doctors formulated their own medicines and patients were forced to pay for them.

Other brutal treatments for insanity were;

- putting patients in a tub with electric eels – the shock was though to be curative
- blood letting, to take away excess blood from the brain
- frightening the patient, for example lowering them in a box drilled with holes into a tub of water. Fear of death was believed to return the brain to a functional state
- spinning the patient fast on a stool to shake the brain together
- cutting out a woman's clitoris, in the that belief sexual organs caused melancholia

Occasionally patients were discharged and given a badge as a license to beg in the surrounding villages. Out of these earnings they were expected to repay the cost of treatment they received in Bethlem.

Early Psychiatry

By the early eighteenth century madness was viewed as a disease of the mind. In 1788 King George III was diagnosed with mental illness and received psychological therapy. A link was being seen between the nervous system, the senses and the intellect. Studies were made of the shaking palsy (epilepsy), tics, hallucinations and aphasia (disturbance of the senses). Phrenology, a study of the personality by examining contours of the brain, was briefly popular before being discredited as unscientific.

The York Retreat 1796

The Quaker William Tuke set up an institution based on moral therapy where patients lived in a hospital-like environment with the staff. He witnessed a fellow Quaker dying in an Asylum and was determined no one should suffer in this way in future. His patients were rewarded for good behaviour and punished for bad in the hope of restoring the mind and were encouraged to study the bible. Mental illness was thought connected to morality.

Tuke's retreat in York is still very active [The Retreat] although not in its original form. It was the fore-runner of a type of retreat, a modern version being 'Maytree' in London where sanctuary is offered over a period of four days for people who feel suicidal.

Victorian Asylums

An 1820 Act of Parliament made it compulsory to have a medically qualified practitioner in attendance at all Asylums. By 1845 every county had to have an Asylum by law. 1890 brought in a new law for two medical certificates to be signed before anyone could be detained in an Asylum. This was to prevent the cruel practice of dumping unwanted relatives [pregnant single women, eccentrics, and so-called moral defectives] in Asylums for personal gain [inheritances] or out of social embarrassment. Such patients were unlikely to be discharged and gradually became institutionalised and forgotten.

The Victorians favoured large institutions so each Asylum held up to 1000 patients. Asylums were very large buildings sited near a village or small town. The acres of land surrounding the Asylum contained special buildings; kitchens, chapels, laundry, industrial units and one or more kitchen gardens. Patients were expected to take up a trade of some kind from shoe making to gardening. Insanity was starting to be de-criminalized and seen as separate from degeneracy but life was still hard for the patients, whose work was expected to pay for their keep. These were not intended to be places for rest and recuperation.

As a matter of interest many famous people were incarcerated in such places including the artist Richard Dadd and William Cowper the poet. King George III (now believed to have suffered arsenic poisoning) was treated for his madness at home where he was restrained by straps during his episodes of illness. Madness never was, nor is, respectful of person, class or wealth.

At the Lincoln Asylum the reformer Robert Gardiner Hill replaced restraints with activity-centred therapy, good diet and exercise. Not surprisingly this regime proved successful. Art and work therapy were available to patients and these are still used therapeutically today.

If you want to see what these places look like inside, try searching: http://www.ukasylums.org.uk/index.asp or try your local Records office. My own photographs of the exterior of St John's Hospital are lodged alongside many others in the Centre for Buckinghamshire Studies in Aylesbury.

1970's - Asylum Life

The Asylums had adapted by late 20th century and were providing housing for severely mentally patients unable to live alone. I met some of these patients whilst doing voluntary work in the 1970's, ladies and gentlemen their 80's and 90's who had lived there all their adult lives having been abandoned by relatives and friends.

One patient was an unmarried mother branded a social misfit. She had her child taken away and her husband divorced her. Another man stole a bicycle when he was a teenager and been 'put away' by his embarrassed parents never to return to his community.

In the 1990's I was case worker to a lovely elderly gentleman (now deceased) who was found in a dishevelled state after his mother died. He was taken to live in a succession of care homes until he was placed in the Asylum. He lived there for 30 years despite the fact he never had an active mental illness. In his final years he often mourned his missed opportunities, a loss which reminds me of the patients Dr Oliver Sachs movingly describes in 'Awakenings'.

One of this man's pet sayings was "*it's a wonderful world*". His last few years were spent living in the community, plodding to the local shops daily to buy the shopping for his group home. I heard many years later that he had been killed in a road traffic accident, a rather poignant ending to his sad life.

Psychosurgery

Phineas Gage - The Rise of Psycho-surgery

In 1848 an event took place which was to radically alter treatment of behavioural disorders.

Phineas Gage, a railroad worker, was exploding rocks with dynamite. A charge went off unexpectedly and a 25mm steel rod was driven (via his cheekbone) into his brain. Immediately after this horrific accident Gage became unconscious and had epileptic fits. Although he survived for 11 years after the accident he underwent a personality change and became very aggressive. It was said by his friends that since the accident Gage had been a different man. Gage's case became famous and he was studied by many eminent doctors of the day.

After his death doctors examined the damaged area of his brain and came to the conclusion that the frontal lobe area (where the damage had occurred) affected personality and mood. His skull was kept for future generations of scientists to study.

Lobotomy

One result of this research was the lobotomy operation. The first lobotomy was carried out by Egas Moniz in 1935 (who won the 1949 Nobel prize for his work).

Unfortunately the procedure was taken up by Walter Freeman who carried out over 2000 operations by sweeping an ice pick back and forth under the brow-ridge of his patients. Nearly 50,000 patients world-wide underwent similar operations in the

1950's and ten per cent died. The operation was not reversible. There is no evidence this brutal practice worked and it was discontinued after 1975. Readers might like to find a copy of the movie 'One Flew Over the Cuckoo's Nest' a moving fictionalised account of a lobotomy. As a footnote, I gather the instigator of this treatment was later paralysed through being shot by a patient whom he lobotomised.

I remember one lady from my volunteer days in a Scottish Asylum who had a lobotomy in the 1950's because of her behavioural problems. The ward sister told me this patient had been "*an intelligent young woman*" but when I knew her she was reduced to a child-like state, wandering the ward weeping as she had done for over 20 years since the operation. I think this ranks among the saddest sights I have seen in the world of mental illness.

In Brief - Talking Cures & Behavioural Therapies

I have given more extensive information about talking cures in a later chapter so will cover it very briefly here.

From early Victorian times, therapists began to understand mental illness in terms of inner mental problems rather than life events. Starting with hypnosis (deep relaxation) and followed by counselling style therapies, treatment began to be less medicine-based. This meant patients no longer had to be monitored frequently and therefore could be treated as day patients in their own communities. The cycle has come full circle, with patients living at home cared for by their families.

Medical Treatments - ECT and Drug Therapy

Again this is a quick romp through modern treatments, as I describe these in later chapters.

ELECTRO-CONVULSIVE THERAPY

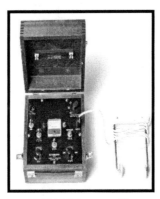

1950's ECT control box

ECT

Patients given sedatives & muscle relaxant
Electrodes attached to each side of the skull
electric current discharged via a control box

Drug Therapy

Drugs given are drugs given orally or by
injection. Anti depressants are synthesised
versions of the brain's
'mood enhancing' chemicals.

Dopamine, noradrenaline and serotonin are the
chemicals responsible for mood change in
depressive illness.

I have already mentioned the early experiments with electric eels by the Romans and in asylums. Modern electro-convulsive therapy (or ECT) was devised as a way of treating shell-shocked soldiers and depressive illness.

Post 1950's a drug called lithium was found effective in treating mania and manic-depressive psychosis. Early anti-psychotic drugs were in common use. Clumsy in effect, these drugs came to be known as liquid coshes because they resulted in patients feeling drowsy and lethargic. However, they were effective in relieving the frightening and dangerous symptoms of psychosis.

The 1960's saw the rise of tranquillisers such as Librium and valium prescribed to generations of women for nerves until they were finally withdrawn from general use as being addictive.

Anti Psychiatric Movement Of 60's And 70's:

Thomas Szaz, R. D. Laing

Some modern Psychiatrists notably Szaz and Laing formed alternative views about mental illness. Laing considered madness a social problem and its symptoms insights.

The anti-psychiatric movement grew as service users, (people who use mental health services) frustrated with the bad effects of the drugs and lack of other treatments, sought answers to their suffering. The books make interesting reading and seen in the light of community treatments make an interesting perspective.

Closure of Asylums & Rise of Psychiatric Hospitals

The NHS & Community Act of the 1990's re-branded Asylums as psychiatric hospitals. The old buildings were closed as former patients went to live in the community in group homes or social housing. I think I mentioned in earlier editions the irony of former crumbling asylums bought up by property developers and refurbished into expensive homes for the same people who so often ignored local 'mental' patients. An example of where the NHS failed to protect its assets by selling the property portfolio.

An average new-build psychiatric hospital might consist of one or two permanent wards, a day hospital and teaching facilities. The advent of effective medication allowed many patients to live in the community returning for treatment during episodes of illness.

Staff worked in community mental health teams comprising mixed disciplines of psychology, occupational therapy, social work, mental nursing and rehabilitation staff. They took on new patients referred by Primary Care [GP surgeries] and discussed care plans for existing patients. Some teams were better lead and organised than others. My experience was unfortunately with not-so-well run teams. Not quite accepted by the medics, being a new profession themselves, nurses could be very unwelcoming to new professionals a cycle I expect will repeat itself as the new grades start to come on board.

A Broader Perspective for Treatment

Patients were now being cared for in psychiatric wards within NHS hospitals, confirming the perception of mental illness as a medical condition (chemical imbalance in the brain). This view is narrow. The more forward thinking movement of the 21st century offers a broader perspective; a wider variety of treatments and listening to patients who are making their voices heard.

These are important milestones in the history of mental health. Mentally ill people are being recognised as capable of making their own decisions. This will have a huge impact on future treatment and on future policies and legislation.

Move Toward Community-Based Care

21st century care is moving towards community care with assertive outreach and emergency duty teams, early interventions for psychosis and more help in surgeries, mopping up long-term patients with frequent relapses. Voluntary organisations such as Samaritans deal with crises such as potential suicides.

There are plans for the complete overhaul of the service which involve a major re-structuring of the work force.

The government needs to put in force the legislation which makes these changes possible without exposing the community to the very few dangerous patients who are a cause for concern.

Virtual Brains - computer simulation

Real hope exists through attempts to build computer-simulated human brains. This will enable faster and accurate research on faulty genes thought to be responsible crippling mental illnesses such as schizophrenia. With this exciting research perhaps we are nearing that time when mental illness will become a thing of the past like polio. I would love to be alive to see this come to fruition.

&&&&&&&&&&&&&

Here are the Greek myths I referred to earlier in this chapter.

In Greek myth, fate is the consequence of family curses passed down through generations until the curse is put to rest, usually with the death of the hero or intervention of a kind god; a bit like Eastenders with attitude. Myths cover the range of human experience and are interesting reading.

The Myth of Oedipus Rex

Laius King of Thebes married Queen Jocasta and they had a son. Hearing from an oracle (wise woman) that the son would kill him Laius had the boy left alone on a mountainside to die. However a shepherd found and adopted the child naming him Oedipus. After many years Oedipus was taken to the King of Corinth who in turn adopted him.

When Oedipus was much older he learned from another oracle that he was destined to kill his father and marry his mother. He had assumed his parents were the shepherd and his wife. Horrified, Oedipus left the palace hoping to escape his fate. On the road to Thebes he quarrelled with an old man and killed him not knowing it was his real father, Laius. After many adventures he rid Thebes of a monster and married the widowed Queen Jocasta not realizing she was his real mother. When they both discovered the mistake Jocasta killed herself and Oedipus put out his own eyes thus fulfilling the oracle.

Freud coined the term Oedipus complex to describe the phenomena of children being sexually attracted to the parent of the opposite sex. He initially dismissed children's reports of parental sexual abuse as being fantasies driven by their Oedipus complex before changing his mind about his theory years later.

&&&&&&&&&&&&&&&&&&&&&&&&

The Myth of the House of Agamemnon

King Agamemnon of Greece was cursed by the gods for the action of an arrogant ancestor. The ancestor had cut his son into pieces and served them at a banquet for the gods in order to test their wisdom. Agamemnon in turn mocked the gods.

The goddess Artemis in revenge forced him to sacrifice his daughter Iphigenia in return for a desperately-wanted victory at the battle of Troy. When Agamemnon returned triumphant from battle he was murdered by his wife Clytemnestra and her lover Aegisthus in revenge for killing Iphigenia. The god Apollo decreed Orestes (son of Agamemnon & Clytemnestra) must put his mother Clytemnestra to death in retribution for the death of the King. Matricide is a mortal sin so Orestes agonised over the god's direction for he knew that the Furies (avenging goddesses) would punish him. Yet, if he did not, he would be disobeying Apollo. Thus he was doomed whatever action he chose to make, a common moral dilemma in Greek myth.

Orestes and his sister Elektra murdered Clytemnestra and Aegisthus. Orestes was inflicted with madness by the Furies until the goddess Athene intervened and the curse of the House of Agamemnon was finally lifted.

"Those whom the gods destroy, they first make mad"
Euripedes

Chapter 2

Defining Sanity & 'Madness'

Contents of this Chapter:

Madness, Sanity, Mental Illness
- A scenario
- Exercise
- Two Small Scenarios
- What does sanity depend upon
- Environment
- Time
- Effect on Other People
- Ability to Survive

Some proposed definitions
Other Triggers of Instability
Stigma and Human Rights

It is easy to assume you know the difference between madness, sanity and mental illness. What is madness? If madness is being out of touch with reality then what is reality? Can you be mentally ill but not insane? In this chapter let's consider these questions. Later in this chapter, I will give you two scenarios to show you how diagnosis works [nb these are for fun - NOT to be considered as proper diagnoses!].

Madness, Sanity, Mental Illness

A man who dreams he is a butterfly. On waking he can't work out if he is a butterfly who has been dreaming he is a man or a man dreaming he is a butterfly. He is confused and has to prove to himself he is a man. If you are interested in this story, read the novel 'The Metamorphosis' by Franz Kafka.

You might laugh at this situation unless you have experienced psychosis. Psychosis is a state of being out of touch with reality.

31

**Madness or Sanity?
The Danger Of Labelling**

Consider these personality traits:

MAD   SPIRITUAL

CREATIVE   **?**   NORMAL

IMAGINATIVE ECCENTRIC

Six people describe an experience. Consider which of the above personality traits most closely fits each person - you can only use each trait once! Answers at foot of page.

Andrew I saw a vision of the Virgin Mary in my room

Maureen I was 7 & Virgin Mary said "happy birthday!"

John I saw the Virgin Mary disguised as a nun

Stella I saw a vision like Virgin Mary outside a Theatre.

Giovanni I had a vision of the Virgin Mary and painted it

Bernie I saw the Virgin Mary in a cave

'Madness' & 'sanity' are meaningless labels.

	Trait	**Explanation**
Andrew	MAD	Andrew was hallucinating
Maureen	IMAGINATIVE	Imagination is good in children
John	ECCENTRIC	John ideas are just eccentric
Stella	NORMAL	Stella is referring to an actress
Giovanni	CREATIVE	Painters often have 'visions'
Bernie	SPIRITUAL	Bernadette is a Catholic saint

During psychosis, patients believe what they are seeing or experience is real. It is somewhat like a nightmare only you are awake and the nightmare continues all the time you are awake. Untreated psychoses are dangerous to the stability of the mind.

The imaginings of madness could be funny, sad, bizarre but are also frightening. The man or woman muttering or laughing in the street may be experiencing psychotic hallucinations. Equally, they may have remembered a funny incident and are responding to it in the way that some people habitually talk to themselves. It is easy for untrained people to assume things.

Madness, as I hope to demonstrate, is a state of mind which exaggerates but mirrors everyday reality. This view is now shared by many professionals.

In time, usually and preferably with medication, psychosis disappears. The hallucinatory world gradually returns to a state of normality like pieces slotting back into a jigsaw puzzle. At a certain point there are enough pieces for the logical part of the brain to take control. The delusions disappear, the chemistry re-balances and sanity returns.

It is at this time that embarrassment or confusion can set in as the recovering person wonders how they acted and what they did during their time of unreality. They may have embarrassed themselves or acted bizarrely in front of family, neighbours or members of their community. This is one reason for the social exclusion of those with episodic [periodic] mental illness. The closest comparable situation is people recovering from drunkenness, high fever or drug taking.

Psychoses use an enormous amount of physical and mental energy which is why people with active mental illness need a long time and quiet space to recuperate.

Mental illness can be experienced in many ways. Episodic illnesses come and go, sometimes people only have one episode during their lifetime. Opposite is the state referred to as 'normal' which is even harder to define. Perhaps we all need a certain frisson of madness to enrich our lives. If you think about it, love is a kind of temporary insanity but that's another book.

You must have read newspapers, books, perhaps surfed the internet. When you look at the global picture there are millions of ethnic and social groups living in different ways - to say nothing of personal individuality or eccentricity. I hope you are beginning to understand how impossible it is to differentiate between mental illness, sanity or eccentricity on a global basis. For example talking about the dead as if they are alive is acceptable to Spiritualists, West Indians, American Indians and some Christian groups but in other circles it is considered bizarre.

We accept children talking about monsters and invisible friends but an adult talking about them is considered eccentric. A writer heard talking to characters from the book they are writing would be considered strange to people who do not know that writers do this commonly.

Let us from now on dispense with the term mad and use the term illness. Madness infers permanent, an illness something treatable.

See what you make of the following incidents. It's a little exercise of imagination.

A scenario

In a busy street you see a scruffily dressed man dressed muttering and gesticulating. Someone calls the police and they arrest him. He resists so they handcuff him and bundle him into a police car. He appears in court next morning, charged as a public nuisance and with resisting arrest.

Exercise

Consider the scenario. Look at the bulleted list below.

List of Characters

1. a Bank Manager
2. a famous actor
3. someone you think may be celebrating a birthday
4. someone who might have cerebral palsy
5. a child under 12 years of age
6. a scowling foreigner carrying a bulky rucksack
7. a man who might be having an epileptic fit
8. a man carrying a sandwich board (advertising board)
9. someone probably under the influence of alcohol or drugs
10. a stranger who is unshaven and wearing ragged clothing
11. a woman with gaudy makeup and clothing

Jot down answers to these questions, for each of the 11 characters:

- is [s]he insane, eccentric or rational
- are you sympathetic to his predicament
- would it influence your view if he was wearing

    a) a suit, or b) ragged clothing

Can you see how easily we make value judgements based on what we think we know or else do not know and are afraid of? Sometimes, its just a matter of clothing or appearance.

I read in a national newspaper last year about a young man ejected from a supermarket by Security Guards on three occasions. They assumed he was a beggar because he was wearing scruffy clothes. In fact he was a charity worker doing his legitimate shopping. He was eventually given public apology by the store management.

Let's return to the courtroom scenario

A first witness in Court is a member of the public who says the man is upsetting people and should be imprisoned.

A second witness is a psychiatrist who diagnoses psychosis. He wants the man detained in a secure hospital.

The Magistrate is about to pronounce sentence when the leader of a street theatre company appears bringing with him three other men wearing costumes. They say the man is one of them, like them he often practices in public. They are angry at his maltreatment. The Magistrate binds the man over to keep the peace and sets him free.

What would YOU have done? I would like you to remember this scenario when I cover the new Mental Health Bill [which has been axed, since writing this].

Two Small Scenarios

You observe the following two men:

The first is wearing a dress, wig and stockings. He is walking in the middle of the road in a seemingly dignified manner brandishing a hardwood stick on top of which is a metal globe.

The second is wearing a red long tunic covered in gold braid and a long curly blonde wig. He is rushing across the road trying to catch papers that are fluttering in the wind. Two policemen are in pursuit. Before looking at the next page* what is your opinion about the two scenarios I have described?

What does sanity depend upon

Environment

The robed man was in a public place acting in what appeared a strange manner. His reactions must be compared with normal behaviour in that community. But behaviour varies depending upon where you are; for example, an arts festival, a formal dinner or a private home.

* ANSWERS

The first is a High Court Judge, heading a parade of dignitaries. The second is a University Chancellor at a graduation ceremony. In our scenario, the wind has blown his papers out of his hand and the police are assisting him. Well done if you got that right.

Imagine a University Chancellor dressed in his ceremonial robes to visit his bank or accountant. Robes are not considered appropriate in those places. However if our Chancellor did wear them he might be thought eccentric. A man in a gorilla suit brandishing a knife with the intent of harming people would be considered ill. The clothing is incidental; the intent to harm is not. Brandishing weapons in public is usually illegal except in a state of war.

Perhaps insanity depends on environment

Time

If the robed man displayed this behaviour over days it would increase the likelihood of his being diagnosed mentally ill. If his behaviour continued for an hour after which he started to behave normally he might be assumed to have a legitimate reason, for example a street actor or eccentric person. Perhaps if our friend the Chancellor kept his robes on all night under the delusion he would be attacked then his wife might legitimately believe he was mentally ill.

Perhaps insanity depends on timing

Effect on Other People

Our muttering friend provoked a series of different reactions. Whilst some people experienced him as benign he appears to have upset others.

Those who were upset wanted him arrested but needless-to-say people who are eccentric are not forcibly treated for their idiosyncrasies unless they live in a totalitarian state.

Perhaps insanity means the effect on others

Ability to Survive

Given this man suddenly appeared on the street at what point would he be considered to be in need of help? If he had not eaten for days or was in danger of being hit by traffic then he might need assistance.

Potential harm to self or others is a consideration

Some proposed definitions

Using examples from my scenarios we could probably say that diagnosis of mental illness means taking into account the following:

- the environment or place where the behaviour is observed
- the period of time the behaviour lasts
- its effect on others
- whether the person poses a danger (to the self or others)

By now you might begin to understand the shifting sand we are treading upon. To be diagnosed with a mental illness has wide reaching consequences for community standing, relationships and employability. I would define a mental illness, as:

that state of mind which permanently or temporarily disables a person from interacting with the everyday world regardless of other considerations such as physical health .

Other Triggers of Instability

Falling in love, bereavement, injustice, loss can all trigger unbalanced states of mind which parallel some of the emotional states experienced by people with active mental illness.

Stigma and Human Rights

You have to take care that, in serving public interest, human rights are not taken away or eccentric behaviour punished or we risk returning to the dark days I described earlier. However, the public must be protected from the few dangerous individuals who undoubtedly need constant watchfulness.

Diagnosis alone can stigmatise. For example, I was offered a job a few years ago only to be turned down at the last moment because I had been honest about my history of depression on the medical form, even though it had not been active for some time.

This kind of thing, from anecdotal evidence, is sadly common practice and needs to be the subject of some kind of human rights legislation otherwise future generations risk long term damage to employment with the ensuing risks for poverty and social isolation.

Patients, Service Users & Carers

".. [a] mentally ill [teenage] female was accused of having sex outside marriage. She was hung. "
Report about a court case in Muslim Iran

Chapter 3

Who Are the 'Mentally Ill' - facts & figures

This chapter contains:

Who Are The 'Mentally Ill'?
Levels of Illness
Mental Illness and Learning Disability
Media and Mental Illness
What Causes Mental Illness
Episodic Nature of Mental Illness
Who Are The 'Mentally Ill'?
Figures

World wide, atrocities are committed daily against people with severe mental illness unable to defend themselves because of their condition and public apathy. In the United Kingdom we are luckier than other societies in that we have the national health service and free treatment.

It is wrong to assume mental illness affects only a small sector of the community. It is not to do with income, intelligence, creativity [although a considerable number of creatives do have mental health problems] or social class.

To scotch another urban myth there are very few people with the kind of personality disorders which might render them dangerous to the public. Most murders are committed by sane people.

Research shows a connection between social deprivation and mental illness but equally it could be triggered by a number of factors including environment, genes, and severe stressors such as bereavement. No one knows the cause as yet, but these are the general opinions. Mental illness is common and becoming more widespread possibly because of the stresses of modern day life.

In this chapter I have included some figures which may surprise you. Depression, for example, is more widespread than asthma.

Levels of Illness

Of course there are many degrees of mental illness from mild anxiety to severe depressive illness, brief psychosis (breakdown experienced after childbirth or during extended periods of severe stress) to enduring mental illnesses such as schizophrenia or manic depression.

Not everyone will categorise illnesses such as anxiety and depression as mental illness but I am doing this for a reason - to normalise these terms and to reduce stigma. If society persists in accepting some illnesses as acceptable and some not, this attitude breeds stigma. For example, we accept that cancer is a common disease [though we fear it]. No one would stigmatise cancer to the extent they would refuse to work with someone with cancer or blame them for getting it.

In mental illness the situation is different. Many people with mental illness are stigmatised, never offered job interviews, refused jobs at the stage of occupational health interview or otherwise castigated because they have been given this label and are considered odd or a threat.

Another absurdity is, the acceptability in polite society of being stressed but not being depressed, or [worse still] to having a diagnosis of schizophrenia or manic depressive psychosis. If we called all mental health problems 'mental illness' or 'brain illness' ('illness' does not imply blame) then that de-stigmatises too. Under the wrong conditions, ANYONE can develop mental illness.

Mental Illness and Learning Disability

Organic brain disease is sometimes confused with mental illness. Organic diseases are very different in that the brain itself is physically damaged. Cerebral palsy is a disorder where the brain is malformed at birth. Alzheimers is a condition in which the brain starts to die with the result of irreversible damage to the personality and memory. Head injuries can affect behaviour and memory permanently or temporarily.

Mind problems cannot be seen because they are not physical injuries. This is what makes diagnosis so difficult.

Media and Mental Illness

Reading newspapers sometimes gives a false impression about mental illness because reporters need to focus on sensational cases in order to sell newspapers. But, you are often reading about the tiny number of people with dangerous personality disorders who commit murder - and of course normal people who are just plain wicked. Wickedness is not mental illness.

There have been many media initiatives backed by organisations such as the Royal College of Psychiatrists to reduce stigma by attempting to report mental illness in a less sensationalist way. One is by not using derogatory terms such as maniac, another by not glamorising suicide and not giving out the method (which discourages copycat suicides).

What Causes Mental Illness

In brief, because this is covered in another chapter, there are many theories. The medical view holds that mental illnesses are caused through chemical problems in the brain. That is why they treat with synthetic versions of the mood brain chemicals (e.g. antidepressants).

Some of these illnesses are thought to be genetic, that is passed on through generations via the genes. A gene thought responsible for schizophrenia has been discovered recently and is under research.

There are many other theories for example:

- holistic models - harmony of mind body spirit
- social and community models - people become ill when they fail to learn social skills

Recurrent mental illness is very much a stroke of fate, or genetics if you like. Just as some people are more prone to asthma or heart disease some are more prone to mental illness. It is nothing to do with moral weakness, low intellect or any of those other urban myths. Depression, in fact, is more common than asthma.

Episodic Nature of Mental Illness

There are treatments which alleviate mental illness but there is no cure. Most mental illnesses are episodic in other words between periods of showing symptoms people with mental illness function as well as anyone else. Anyone, your bank manager, doctor, accountant, postman, might be receiving treatment for mental illness and you would never know it in this age of anti-psychotics and antidepressants.

Have a look at some of these facts and figures and begin to think about your own reactions to what you have read so far.

Figures / Statistics

Note: Crown copyright material is reproduced with the permission of the Controller of HMSO and the Queen's Printer for Scotland.

Male suicides, trend from 1974 to 2000

The chart shows numbers per 100,000 of population. It can be seen that, although the trend is downwards, suicides among young men are increasing.

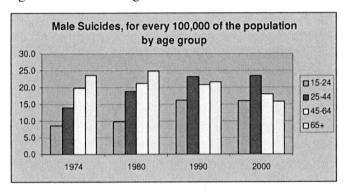

Female suicides, trend from 1974 to 2000

This chart represents deaths by suicide per 100,000 of population. The downward trend can be seen except among youngsters.

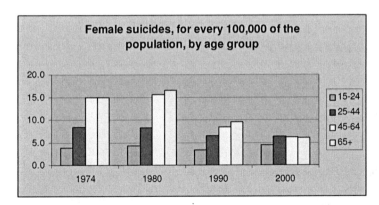

One of the ways in which the Government is attempting to address this issue is by media initiatives in magazines likely to be read by these age groups, and in schools.

The chart below chart shows the **male to female suicides** by proportion in 2000 (the latest statistics) showing male suicides predominating over female suicides by nearly three quarters.

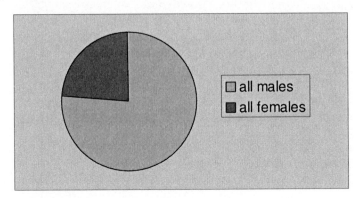

all males
all females

Mental Illness and Stigma

Following are some interesting facts about mental illness and stigma. I prepared the pie charts from the 2003 report of the Office for National Statistics, 'Attitudes to Mental Illness'. The figures were taken from a poll of ordinary people, in order to see if there have been any changes in attitude over the last few years. These figures show a considerable reduction in stigma. For the sake of space, I have only shown the latest survey [2003].

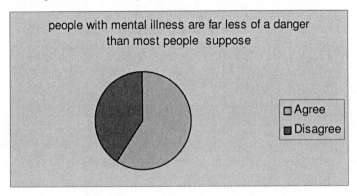

people with mental illness are far less of a danger than most people suppose

Agree
Disagree

Nearly 33% of people would not want someone who has been mentally ill to live next door to them. With 1:4 people suffering a mental illness at some time in their lives, this is an unrealistic expectation!

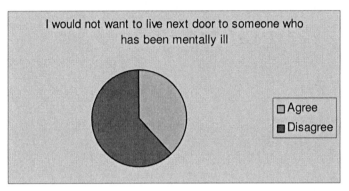

Most people agree that anyone can become mentally ill and this is now proven as you can see from the chart below. This is another proof that stigma is being successfully reduced by these new measures.

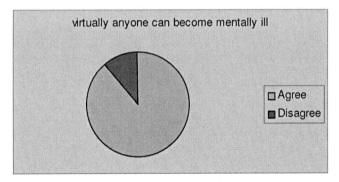

Nearly 3% felt that people with mental health problems should **not** have the same rights to work as everyone else. This is quite mortifying.

Lack of work leads to poverty and isolation - all of these proven factors in the onset of mental health problems.

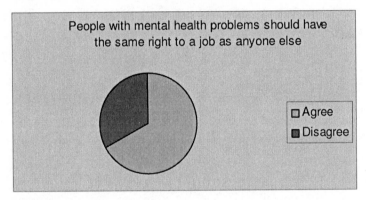

A huge proportion of the people polled knew a relative, friend or even themselves had experienced mental illness so knowledge seems to be increasing.

Astonishingly, nearly 25% felt that someone who had had a mental illness should be excluded from public office.

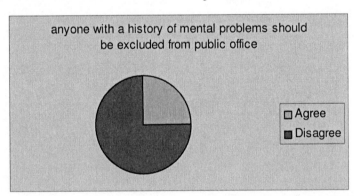

There is still a division between those who feel the public still need protecting from certain kinds of person with mental illness. But, more people do believe these dangers are exaggerated. I have not included this chart but many people failed to correctly answer how many people they thought would developed a mental illness. Fewer than 7% thought it 1 in 10; some guessed at 1 in 1000. The correct figure is 1 in 4. Rather a sobering thought is it not?

This sort of data is vital for the Government to be able to quantify the effects of its anti-stigma and social inclusion policies in order to target specific areas.

Many statutory and voluntary agencies are currently working to reduce stigma and educate the public, including the major mental health charities, Royal College of Psychiatrists, Care Services Improvement Partnership [of which NIMHE, the National Institute for Mental Health in England, is now a part].

*"It is a tragic irony...that so many carers are forced into
poverty and isolation"*
Diana Whitworth, Carers UK Chief Executive

Chapter 4

Service Users & Carers

This Chapter Contains:

Service Users
Carers
Lack of information
Carer Surgeries
Emotional Response of Carers
• Lack of help
• Employment Considerations
• Isolation
Young Carers Problems
Carers organisations

Service Users

This might be a curious title for anyone outside the mental health
profession, but it is one of many politically correct titles given to
people who actively use mental health services. Myself, I prefer
patient. Patient implies short term treatment for specifics whereas
service user, consumer, client imply longer term relationships.

Carers

A carer is a person who voluntarily cares for another. It is
estimated there are 5.7 million family carers in Britain (1995
Carers UK survey). Of these 399,000 care for someone with
mental illness and 855,000 for someone with mental and physical
illnesses. It is no wonder a conservatory estimate of *£34billion
per year is saved by the NHS on professional care.

*note: Carers UK, secondary source Inst. Of Actuaries Report 1993

There are carers of all ages including those regarded as children in law. In 2002 the NSPCC estimated up to 12% of adults have a psychiatric problem and have to be cared for by their children which is quite shocking.

Three sets of families were interviewed during a recent excellent BBC Radio 4 programme (Caring Beyond Reason, 8pm 9th March 2006] talked about their experiences. The programme was poignant without being mawkish.

This is the URL (web address) if you would like to listen to that programme [the site was live as this book goes to print] http://www.bbc.co.uk/radio4/science/pip/c1oam/

Lack of Information

Lack of information about the nature and course of mental illness is of great concern for carers. I have seen patients whose family are making the situation worse by ill-thought out comments (including the common phrase 'try and pull yourself together').

Mental illness is difficult to understand because there are no physical symptoms. Even 21st century technology is only just starting to pinpoint faulty genes which may cause mental illness but this is in its infancy. The best clue is behaviour or mood changes but even these can be misinterpreted. Unusually moody, possibly high-spirited or aggressive? These characteristics could be temperament or changes due to physical illness. Teenagers are notoriously moody but this is may be normal and not a sign of impending mental illness.

Even if a serious problem requiring hospitalisation occurs try explaining the ins and outs to a distraught ill-informed parent who is facing a team of heavy guys about to forcibly section a much loved and usually quiet son, daughter or granny.

With the advent of the Internet, the voices of mental health charities and better media cover, there is much more information available. American sites are particularly helpful as there is not as much stigma in the USA.

There is the problem of false information which spreads easily on the Internet. Sticking to '.ac' [university] sites or those connected with respected journals, charities and professional organisations would be wise when seeking information from unknown sites.

Carer Surgeries

My solution would be state-funded carer surgeries in local areas where carers could meet with trained educators in a social setting. There would need to be provision for the cared-for person to be looked after during such surgeries. These problems are not insurmountable. There are vast savings on care because family carers provide their services free of charge. Provision of basics like rooms would be a welcome gesture.

Emotional Response of Carers

Caring for someone 24 hours a day drains emotions. Imagine having a problem that cannot be resolved and that problem faces you day and night. Carers go through this year in and year out. I saw the parents of a young lady with major mental illness nearly driven insane because they regularly experienced her gradual deterioration to the point of hospitalisation. The constant watchfulness and sleepless nights took a huge toll on this elderly couple.

Lack of help

There are small amounts of respite care. Sometimes it is a relief for a relative to be sectioned as it gives the carer a break. Young carers need a regular break away with people of their own age. The amount of money available for caring is minimal and there are hoops to go through before grants are given. It would be easier for carers to refuse to perform their service but in practice I doubt many carers would refuse. This moral obligation delegates the entire burden from a social to personal responsibility.

Employment Considerations

A large proportion of carers cannot go out to work because they can only offer limited hours without a sitter to look after their relative. Employers are hardly likely to be sympathetic. Carers have little income or energy with which to study. This leaves them in a similar problem to those with mental illness. Massive funding would be required to redress the employability situation but there are ways which could be considered, including:

- computers being made available to carers free of charge
- office link-ups enabling carers to work from home
- co-operative schemes run by carers organisations

Isolation

Isolation is a tremendous problem. Carers who cannot get out and who have little spare income have few social opportunities. If your day is filled with the problems of being a carer that becomes an issue in itself, for few people want to listen to problems. There are two areas of contact required; one with professionals who will listen and one on a social basis.

Young Carers Problems

Children and adolescents who care for mentally ill parents over a long period experience a variety of problems including:

- abuse – physical or mental
- loss of security
- loss of educational opportunity
- emotional damage
- bullying at school and work
- loneliness
- social and behavioural difficulties

The experience of caring for a mentally ill parent is difficult to describe. The behaviours learned under those circumstances do not fit what is accepted as normal at school and these youngsters become excluded without knowing why. Such children are often bullied at school.

As with other carers, young carers can find difficulty when it comes to study. It is hard to learn when you are emotionally drained and have domestic duties at home. Social and behavioural problems follow as the child begins unwittingly to follow the social and behavioural patterns of the parent.

These difficulties can haunt both adolescence and the working years. The bonus is, such children are often voracious for knowledge and can find great comfort in academia, sport and creative pursuits when early life problems have been resolved.

Carers organisations

There are many carers organisations the most prominent of which is Carers UK which has many local branches. These organisations exist to fight carers rights, to publicise the problems associated with caring and to prove a forum for discussion. Local branches provide support groups and local information.

The Medical Model

The Human Brain

This beautiful image is an enhanced 3D model of neurones [brain nerve cells].The image has been improved for clarity. The brain contains a mass of interconnected fibres.
The synapses [hair-like filaments] surround each cell but do not touch. Your brain contains billions of such cells. Brain activity can be seen on an EEG [electro-encephalograph] machine

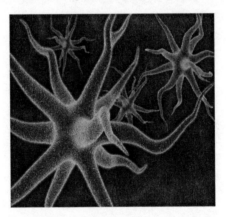

Brain cells are connected chemically through 'neurotransmitters' - chemicals such as dopamine, serotonin & nor-adrenaline. These are produced naturally in the brain. The chemicals distribute themselves by 'firing' across gaps between cells [similar to electric charge jumping the gaps in a car's sparking plug].

Neurotransmitters are responsible for mood levels. If there is poor distribution of these in the brain, the result might be a depressed mood. If there is too much activity, this could indicate mania.

No one knows exactly how this process works. Brain chemistry can take between 6 months and a year to re-balance. If this fails to happen [which is very rare] then antidepressants need to be administered permanently.

"Drug companies.. encouraged the idea that mental illnesses are caused by imbalance of brain chemicals (even 'invented' illnesses to go with the drugs)"
Prof C H Ashton

Chapter 5

Medical View - Chemical Imbalances

Contents of this chapter:

The Medical Model
The Function of the Human Brain
Memory and Recall
Imbalance of Brain Chemistry
• What Causes A Chemical Imbalance in the Brain?
• How Are These Imbalances Treated?
British Neurological Association

The Medical Model

The medical model is the theory on which doctors base their treatments. In the medical model, mental illness is thought to be caused by an imbalance of chemicals in the brain. What causes this imbalance is a complex question not fully answered.

In order to explain this section it is necessary to understand what is going on inside that grey spongy mass we call the human brain. If you refer to the illustration in this chapter, it should make things clearer.

The Function of the Human Brain

There are billions of cells in the brain. Each cell is a separate entity although there are masses of fibres in the brain. Each cell is surrounded by long filaments called synapses. There is a picture of these opposite. Along the length of these filaments are tentacle-like suckers. These trailing fibres are not long enough to join the cells but rather cleverly the brain is designed to deal with this problem otherwise we would all be permanently brain-dead. Imagine each octopus-like synapse firing chemicals at each other. It is this charge of chemicals which join the brain cells together. It's a bit like star wars inside your brain.

The chemicals they are firing are dopamine, noradrenaline and serotonin, the so called mood-enhancing chemicals which enable you to experience a normal range of moods. Remember these names and you can impress your GP.

You can see the effect of this activity on the readout of an electro-encephalograph (EEG) machine. An EEG is a brain scanner in the same way that an electro-cardiograph (ECG) is a heart scanner.

Ah, you might ask, if we all have the same chemistry, then why are our moods so different? Why does Mrs Jones cry more than Mr Smith; or Mr James never seem as if he has any feelings? The answer to that lies in our genes. We are individuals born with different natural capacity for experiencing emotion. However, we all have a range of normal moods (or what passes for normal).

Memory and Recall

As well as looking after your mental welfare the synapses of the brain cells carry the elusive elements of memory and recall. You can improve your memory by exercising it which causes more and more of the synapses to form. The more you use it the less you lose it. So mental gymnastics really do work which is why people are encouraged to do mental exercises such as crosswords or reading more as they get older (must make a mental note to do this myself). Read Tony Buzan's books on memory.

For passing interest, readers might have seen a recent Channel 5 documentary called 'the woman with no brain'. This was a

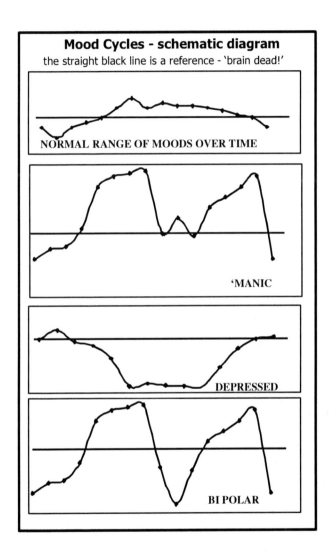

Mood Cycles - schematic diagram
the straight black line is a reference - 'brain dead!'

NORMAL RANGE OF MOODS OVER TIME

'MANIC

DEPRESSED

BI POLAR

Fascinating programme about a woman with encephalitis. Brain fluid filled the area where her brain should have been leaving a large hole which should clearly be seen on a scan. Astonishingly brain fibres started to grow around this hole and she was able to live a normal family life with no apparent loss of intellect or memory. Proof of the body's astonishing ability to heal itself. But I digress..

Imbalance of Brain Chemistry

The medical theory works like this. If there is not enough mood enhancing chemical in the brain then the result is depressed mood. Too much and the mood will be excessively elated (manic or high). These mood changes are reversible as the chemistry re-balances itself, usually with the help of medication.

What Causes A Chemical Imbalance in the Brain?

No one knows what causes this imbalance of chemicals. Some clinicians believe it is hormonal changes in the body others a symptom of faulty genes. However, there are many other theories of a non-chemical kind which some medical people accept:

- taking illegal drugs
- excessive alcohol intake
- birthing problems (post-partum depressive illness)
- genetic factors (genes passed by parents to their children)
- brain injury
- environmental factors e.g. poverty, poor housing, severe stress

How Are These Imbalances Treated?

The cause suggests the cure. Chemicals can be artificially introduced through drug therapy. Drugs are combinations of chemicals, designed for specific purposes. In severe cases a method called electro convulsive therapy (ECT) is sometimes used although this is becoming controversial and is no longer recommended by the National Institute of Clinical Excellence [NICE] as a treatment of choice except in severe cases.

Drugs are prescribed for a period of between 6 months and a year. Eventually, in most cases, the brain starts to produce enough chemical transmitters and medication is discontinued. Again, no one knows why or how this process happens.

If medication is stopped prematurely this natural healing will not have taken place and the low or high moods return. This is why some people claim medication does not work.

British Neurological Association

As neurology is a relatively new science lack of knowledge is one of the frustrations but also one of the most exciting things about it. There remain many discoveries to be made. Which is where I shall give a plug to the British Neurological Association who kindly gave me a copy of their excellent book 'Neuroscience: Science of the Brain. An Introduction for Young Students'. Never mind the young students, it's a very good read. Your son or daughter or grandchild might gain a lifetime fascination for the brain and become a pioneer. Can't be bad for a few pounds.

"the tendency of newly qualified therapists to see in every patient the disease they are currently studying"
Clinical tutor

Chapter 6

Medical - 'Detection to Diagnosis'

This chapter contains:

Cultural Issues
How Mental Illness is Detected
* Presenting for Treatment
* Primary Care
* Community Mental Health Team
* Direct Referral to Social Services
How Diagnoses are Made
Case History
* Physical Examination
* The Diagnosis
* The Diagnostic Manual
Undisclosed Cases of Mental Illness

One of the junior psychiatrists I worked with was thumbing through DSMIV, the diagnostic textbook. He remarked that according to what was he was reading all the staff would qualify for some kind of treatment. He was not far wrong. Diagnosis is difficult.

Cultural Issues

There is no standard human being with specific feelings, beliefs and behaviours. This is why it is difficult to detect all but the most severe of mental illnesses. What passes for normal in one family could be considered abnormal in another.

Taking cultural factors into consideration is vital in making diagnoses. For example West Indians and Spiritualists believe visitations of ghosts and spirits to be normal whilst generally in

European culture someone who talks about ghosts might be thought hallucinating (seeing things which are not there). In the past, diagnoses have been made incorrectly through cultural ignorance for example assuming someone talking of spirits has a schizophrenia-like illness.

So how is a medical mental health diagnosis made, and at what point do unusual experiences become diagnosable as medical symptoms?

How Mental Illness is Detected

Two of the first signs of mental illness are marked differences in behaviour or mood. These changes could take place over days, months or even years. There is no fixed time about the onset of mental illness. However the longer the symptoms are untreated the worse they can become.

Difficulties might take many forms for example extreme tiredness or increased energy; memory problems; difficulty concentrating; irritability or tearfulness; changes in moral or social standards, such as a timid woman becoming promiscuous or a lively person sliding into a dark mood. You might notice problems in carrying out a normal workload at work or home. These changes would be outside the person's usual set of behaviours. However, that is not to be confused with legitimate life reasons for personality change for example a quiet person wins the lottery, someone falls in love and becomes exhilarated or even sulky or belligerent.

Anxiety and stress are considered common risks of daily life, but when they become intolerable then some kind of intervention is required. Everyone, to paraphrase Topol in the 'Fiddler on the Roof', deserves some kind of happiness. Medication is not usually given unless symptoms are severe or long lasting and the patient find it difficult to enjoy or cope with their daily life or becomes a danger to themselves or others.

Presenting for Treatment

Remember this chapter is concerned with medical treatments and I will cover other treatments later. In the 21st century there has been a huge shift in attitude towards the treatment of mental health problems and medical treatments.

So how do these people arrive at the place where they can receive medical help? Well, that depends upon the type and severity of symptoms and on the culture and beliefs of the person presenting.

Primary Care

Anyone who feels that life is getting on top of them can present themselves to their G.P. surgery [Primary Care]. Some patients present with physical symptoms, but as every wise G.P. knows mind and body are connected and affect each other. Heart problems, back pain, psoriasis (skin eruptions), colds, weight problems - an endless list of symptoms with combined physical and mental causes.

In most cases G.P.s both diagnose mental health problems and dispense psychiatric drugs. They might refer the patient to someone within the surgery such as a Counsellor, Health Nurse, Family Worker or perhaps for psycho-educational training (increasingly popular). Some psychotherapy is offered in the NHS but there are very long waiting lists.

It is usual for patients with more severe symptoms such as severe depression, schizophrenia, obsessive compulsive disorder or psychosis to be referred for psychiatric assessment.

Community Mental Health Team

Psychiatrists are doctors who have taken specialist training in prescribing psychiatric medication. Patients do not self refer to a CMHT unless they have recurring mental illness and are already known to the service.

The worker assigned to the patient reports back to the team. If someone needs to be sectioned under the current Mental Health Act then an assessment by 2 doctors (usually psychiatrists) has to be made before the necessary papers can be signed. The process of sectioning is explained further in the chapters on the Mental Health Act and Bill.

Direct Referral to Social Services

Relatives worried about severe mental symptoms being displayed by a member of their family can call an emergency duty G.P. or refer direct to Social Services. In the former case, the G.P. might arrange an emergency referral to CMHT. In the latter case a Social Worker will call to the family home to assess the situation. These days, Approved Social Workers work within a Community Mental Health Team rather than Social Services although they remain employed by them.

If the Social Worker considers the person in need of immediate treatment (that is, a potential suicide or homicide risk) then that person can be sectioned under the Mental Health Act. Under the current Act all treatment is carried out in a psychiatric setting.

How Diagnoses are Made

What follows is a description of how a medical diagnosis is made by a psychiatrist or less commonly by G.P.s. There is still a stigma attached to mental illness, a matter I will discuss in the case studies section therefore doctors have to be careful how they present their findings to patients and relatives.

My dictionary defines diagnosis as *"identification of disease by* [an] *investigation of symptoms and history"*. The aim of a diagnosis is to put a name to a condition so that it can be treated more easily. No one likes being labelled with a diagnosis as such but putting a name to a condition makes it easier to establish symptoms, causes, and potential cures.

Case History

A case history enables the patient to tell their story and the listening clinician makes conclusions. This does not happen in one session, but may take several appointments.

The professional is looking for;

1. the chain of events which lead to the illness
2. if they have had similar reactions before
3. family health history, both physical and mental
4. changes in mood and /or behaviour
5. how they are feeling now

These questions will enable the professional to establish:

1. where the problems might have started
2. how well the patient is able to deal with life generally
3. if there is a history of similar illness in the family
4. how long the illness has been affecting the patient
5. how serious the current problem is

Physical Examination

The patient might undergo blood or psychological tests or be given a physical examination which will help determine what the illness is and the severity of the problem. For example a blood test might indicate high levels of lithium in the blood a chemical known to be a factor in mania.

The Diagnosis

Finally, the professional is ready to apply all that [s]he has discovered in the course of testing and make a diagnosis. A diagnosis is the end product of a medication examination. Psychiatrists often use the diagnostic manual (see below) as a guideline.

The Diagnostic Manual

One of the tools a professional might use is a book called 'The Diagnostic and Statistics Manual' (DSM) the current version being DSM IV. This is an American publication (American Psychiatric Association) and is used world wide for diagnosis.

In this manual there are lists of the criteria (conditions) for a huge range of mental conditions. It is a kind of service manual which tells medical people what to look for; a bit like the service manual used by your mechanic to diagnose faults in a car.

DSM IV gives a range of severity for symptoms. The guidelines are precise and based on years of observation and research. Each mental condition has a set of numbers and letters (called keys) allowing the professional to diagnose in a systematic way.

If you look at my chapter on case histories, you will notice that I have listed the symptoms for each of a range of mental health disorders. These are from DSM IV. Although this manual is useful professionals also apply knowledge from their professional experience.

Undisclosed Cases of Mental Illness

Mental illnesses can only be diagnosed if episodes are brought to the attention of a professional. It may seem obvious but there are probably millions of cases which never come to the attention of a professional, perhaps because:

- family or friends might tolerate odd behaviour
- an abnormal family considers itself normal
- depressive illness seen as normal life sadness
- mania might be seen as extreme high spirits
- the person might be cared for within their own culture
- illness would not be noticed in a person living alone

I hope you can appreciate why it is so important for diagnoses to be made with caution and how difficult this process is for both doctors and patients. With more extensive knowledge of mental illness and less stigma the balance is now changing as mental wellness becomes an acceptable part of everyday life. This can only be a change for the better.

So, having made the diagnosis, how is the patient to be treated for their condition? Let's take a look at some of the treatments in the medical practitioner's armoury.

"[Nobody] wants to stay on medication for years .. it can help .. people lead the lives they want to lead"

Mental Health Organisation

Chapter 7

Drug Therapy, E.C.T. & Psychosurgery

Contents of This Chapter:

Drug Therapies
- What are Drugs
- Why Is DrugTherapy Sometimes Considered Immoral?
- Patient Compliance With Drug Therapy
- Categories of Drugs for Sale
- Natural Drugs
- Manufactured Drugs
- Antidepressants
- SSRI's (Specific Serotonin Re-Uptake Inhibitors)
- MAOI's (monoamine oxidase inhibitors)
- Tricyclics
- SSRI's (Selective Serotonin Re-Uptake Inhibitors)
- Antipsychotics
- Antimanics

Some Moral Issues of Medication
Common Side Effects of Drugs
Electro Convulsive Therapy (ECT)
- Delivery of Electro Convulsive Therapy
- Is ECT Effective?
- NICE Report on ECT

Psychosurgery
Battery Operated Brain Pacemaker Pack

In this chapter I will endeavour to explain some of the medical treatments on offer for mental illness: electro convulsive therapy (ECT), drug therapies (medications), psychosurgery and also a very new treatment called DBS (deep brain stimulation).

Drug Therapies

What are Drugs

Drugs or medications are combinations of chemicals synthesised by pharmaceutical companies to treat specific illnesses. I'll describe how new drugs come onto the market in a later chapter.

Qualified medical practitioners (G.P.s, consultants, psychiatrists and some specially trained nurses) can prescribe drugs. It is estimated that 25% of medicines prescribed are for psychiatric conditions (report by SANE).

Drugs can be both curative and harmful. Morphine, heroin and cocaine become illegal and harmful when they are supplied or used by people unqualified to prescribe or be prescribed to. In medicine all these drugs are used for pain relief.

- antidepressants relieve low moods of depressive illness
- antipsychotics prevent hallucinations & delusions

Why Is Drug Therapy Sometimes Considered Immoral?

Unlike other treatments psychiatric drugs affect both emotions and behaviour. That is how they work. People are often afraid of taking these drugs, because they fear it will change their personality or render them unable to think and feel properly.

Some research points to the fact that older people are vulnerable to over-prescription of psychotic medication. Antipsychotic medicines have a calming effect and it must be tempting to prescribe rather than deal with demanding aged patients.

Totalitarian states are well documented for administering medication to all who oppose the regimes rendering these forced patients into stupor like states and in some cases killing them. One cannot imagine psychiatrists willingly prescribing in this way although there are Shipman-like rogues in every profession.

Patient Compliance with Drug Therapy

I can understand the fears around dulling of the senses. Some drugs, particular earlier types, did indeed dull the emotions and make patients feel as if they had been hit with a brick; the 'emotional cosh' sensation many describe. They also have the effect of rendering people really weary, as if the weariness of the original illness were not enough.

These are some of the reasons patients do not take prescribed medication:

- fear of loss of control of humanity
- fear of psychological dependence
- fear through lack of explanation about the drugs
- fear of loss of creativity or drive - emotional flatness
- in psychosis - fear of poison or an attempt to control
- in depression - belief that recovery is not possible
- in mania - enjoyment of mania or fear of depression
- forgetfulness
- side effects being worse than the benefits
- as the drugs start to work, patients may wrongly assume the brain chemistry is functioning and stop taking medication before the natural brain chemistry balance is restored

It may be hard for patients to explain these reasons to clinicians. Busy doctors might reach for the prescription pad rather than asking the patient what they want and offering other options. Thanks to more patient choice this is slowly changing, particularly with green prescriptions.

Categories of Drugs for Sale

Some of the drugs in a chemist's shop are prescription only and cannot be dispensed unless a chemist is present. The Medicines Act 1968 lays down guidelines about which medicines can or cannot be sold over the counter.

DRUG CATEGORIES
Drugs & Herbs

Valium   Diazapam

............................CHAMOMILE

SEDATIVES
[Barbiturates
beta blockers   Secobarbita
hypnotics]

VALERIAN
depress' nerves
• diminish anxiety
• reduce paranoia
• reduce aggression

Librium   **Treatment of:**
• convulsions
• insomnia

Readers are always recommended to consult a medical practitioner before taking any kind of remedy.

Largactil   **ANTI** Clozaril.
PSYCHOTICS
(major tranquillisers)
[reduce hallucinations]

Melleril   Serdolect
Treatment of:
• psychoses
• hallucinations
• mania
• schizophrenia

Distalgesic   Tylenol

COMFREY
ANALGESICS
Decrease pain
MARIGOLD
aspirin
Treatment of:
• headache
• physical pain

MEADOWSWEET   Seroxat

SAGE
ANTI DEPRESSANTS
[type of tranquilliser]
• improves mood
• relieve emotional pain

Gamanlil   Prozac
Treatment of:
• anxiety
• depressive illness
• sleeplessness

CINNAMON   FENNEL
caffeine
STIMULANTS
• stimulate nerves
• increase wakefulness
• loss of appetite
amphetamines
Treatment of:
• tiredness

72

Drugs are divided legally into four classes, described on a leaflet inside a box of medication:

- **POM** - prescription only; can be sold only on prescription
- **GSL** - general sale list; can be sold over-the-counter
- **P** - Pharmacist; can be sold only when pharmacist is present
- **CDPOM** - controlled drug prescription; dangerous drugs with stringent guidelines for sale and use. Prescription must be in the GP's handwriting

Natural Drugs

The diagram in this chapter is an attempt to categorise types of medications which act upon the nervous system. Although this is the medical therapy part of my book you will notice I have listed some of the plants used in holistic therapies. Plants, roots, bark and berries were used as medicines for thousands of years before the pharmaceutical industries started producing synthesised versions of natural remedies. Some modern drugs are still made directly from plant materials rather than laboratory grown chemicals. The following plants are examples of the origin of many useful remedies still in medical use:

- curare; poisonous herb used as muscle relaxant in surgery
- belladonna (deadly nightshade); dilates pupils in eye operations
- digitalis (foxglove); used to regulate heart beats
- amaryllis belladonna; relief of Alzheimer's disease
- valeriana officinalis (valerian); a sedative
- myrrhis odorata (sweet cicely); on trial as anti-cancer drug
- mentha spicata (spearmint); calming nervous disorders
- envallaria majatis (lily of the valley); antispasmodic and diuretic
- salix purpurea (purple osier); origin of 'aspirin' [bark]
- asarum canadense (wild ginger); used for head colds
- tanacetum parthenium (feverfew); used for migraine relief

If you look at these herbs in any Botanic Garden you will be awestruck by the beauty and diversity of the plants. Some of them have been used for thousands of years as natural curatives especially in Chinese herbal medicine, homeopathy and folk remedies. Some of the most powerful drugs currently on the market are extracted from roots, leaves, bark and flowers. The only difference is, where laboratories extract the active ingredients patients can be more sure of the exact dilution than if the plants are digested directly. This controlled dilution is vital in the more potentially lethal herbs.

There was an interesting programme on this topic recently (31st January 2006 BBC2 9 to 10pm 'Alternative Medicine, The Evidence' presented by Professor Kathy Sykes. Professor Sykes was discussing herbal remedies with a biochemist and we learned that chemists still do not know why some plants are effective medicines across a diverse range of conditions.

Many contain multiple chemicals which, working together, have different properties than their individual chemical components. Scientists call this process of 'the whole being greater than the sum of the parts' or synergy [some call this complexity]. Synergy is what makes it so difficult to reproduce the chemical properties of therapeutically effective plants. An exciting area for research.

Manufactured Drugs

Let's look at the kinds of psychiatric medication currently on the market. By the way, the term 'psychiatric medication' means medicine which acts upon the mind. It does not have the more sinister connotation given by certain works of fiction or movies.

There are 3 main groups of drugs which act upon the nervous system:

- sedatives – sedate
- stimulants – stimulate
- analgesics – act as pain killers

For the purposes of this book, we are only concerned with the first category of sedatives (antidepressants, antipsychotics, anti-manics).

The Neurotransmitters

It is useful to reconsider the purpose of the neurotransmitters. As the name suggests neurotransmitters deliver mood-changing chemicals to the synapses (remember these? Tiny hair-like structures around each nerve cell). It is thought depressive illness is caused by the brain producing insufficient neurotransmitter to stimulate the nerve cells.

Imagine the brain cells as a cable, the chemical transmitters as an electric current and the brain as a light bulb. If there is sufficient electrical current (serotonin) pushed through the cable the light bulb will work. If there is a dip or surge on the current the bulb will either dim [suppress - depression] or glow brighter [excite – mania].

For the less technically minded among you, imagine two people playing badminton. The people are the brain cells, the bats the transmitters and the shuttlecocks the chemical transmitter. So the cells are effectively joined by the shuttlecocks but if there is no shuttlecock [or feathers are missing], game over; dead brain.

Antidepressants

Antidepressants counteract the symptoms of depressive illness. There are many types on the market with different properties, but generally they:

- relieve emotional pain
- promoting sleep
- increase/curb appetite
- reduce anxiety

Sometimes antidepressants are prescribed for anxiety disorders but that is not their manufactured purpose. Incidentally, pharmacists are actually more qualified than G.P.s where drug therapies are concerned as that is their specialism. Changes are being planned in the legislation which will allow pharmacists to prescribe as well as dispense.

There are three kinds of antidepressants:

- Tricyclics
- SSRI's (Specific Serotonin Re-Uptake Inhibitors)
- MAOI's (monoamine oxidase inhibitors)

Tricyclics

Scientists believe that another reason for the low moods of depression is too much of the neurotransmitter being broken down in the natural process by an enzyme called monoamine oxide.

Tricyclic antidepressants increase the number of natural chemical transmitters by preventing the monoamine oxide from absorbing them.

The medication has to be taken over months, perhaps years, in order to build up the quality of transmitter in the brain. Tricyclic refers to chemical structure of the drug which resembles 3 rings (structurally like the rings on the flag of the Olympic Games).

Tricyclics are old-fashioned and not generally prescribed now as they are not as effective as the SSRI's, which very conveniently come next.

Examples of tricyclic antidepressants: Imipramine, Amitriptyline

SSRI's (Selective Serotonin Re-Uptake Inhibitors)

Serotonin is a neurotransmitter. SSRI's are designed to increase the amount of serotonin in the brain chemistry by blocking the natural enzyme which destroys them. Re-uptake means re-absorb.

Examples of SSRI's: Prozac, Faverin, Seroxat

MAOI's (monoamine oxidase inhibitors)

The amount of monamines in the body controls the fluctuation of mood (monamines destroy the neurotransmitters as part of the natural process in the brain).

MAO inhibitors are designed to prevent a build-up of the monamine enzyme. MAOI's are not used widely because they interact badly with a variety of other drugs.

Example of MAOI: Marplan, Parnate, Manerix

Antipsychotics

Antipsychotic medication relieves the symptoms of:

* schizophrenia
* psychosis within a clinical depression
* psychosis in manic depressive illness
* brief psychotic disorder

These drugs help prevent auditory and visual hallucinations, delusions, disorganised thinking and obsessions. They basically dampen down over-responsive nerve cells.

There are many different kinds of antipsychotic medication:

* Largactil (from the chemical chorpromazine)
* Dozic, Haldol, Serenace (from the chemical haloperidol)

Among the newer types of antipsychotics are some which have reduced side effects are:

* Clozaril (clozapine)
* Risperdal (risperidone) - an expensive drug, and one which concerns the scientists in the U.S.
* Serdolect (sertindole)

New drugs are coming onto the market all the time so being a non chemist I cannot quote all the latest drugs on the market but you can easily look them up. There are many books and websites about psychiatric medications which are written for lay people.

Antimanics

Episodes of mania and manic depressive psychosis are treated with antipsychotics to reduce the mania, then ongoing lithium therapy. Lithium salts are toxic and clinicians have to carry out regular blood tests to make sure the amount of lithium in the blood is stabilised. Lithium levels out the mood and is taken continuously to prevent further episodes of illness.

Some Moral Issues of Medication

Medication enables people to hold down jobs and live reasonably stable lives. The bank clerk or shop girl in your community might have active schizophrenia and you would never know. Symptoms can be controlled by drugs. But there is a price.

All drugs have unwanted side affects. Long term medication for psychosis can cause unwanted shaking called parkinsonism, or tardive dyskinesia (constant rolling of the tongue and smacking the lips). Such mannerisms mark people out and they can be subjected to ridicule. Medication can also cause considerable weight-gain with the consequent loss of self-confidence.

New drugs come onto the market frequently and it is debatable if pharmaceutical companies are using patients as living guinea pigs on what amounts to a massive ongoing drug trial.

Anyone can look at the list of side effects but not know which ones they will experience. Brain medication touches the root of the psyche and many people fear changes which affect the mind. Patients can fear losing emotional responses and potential changes to their character or temperament. These are genuine fears, because you need to remember that taking psychiatric drugs is not like taking an aspirin; it is more on the scale of an anti-cancer drug.

Some patients need to take a cocktail of preparations and are doomed to continue this regime until advancing scientific knowledge comes up with an alternative. I cannot imagine what it must be like for patients who have to control mania with lithium. Lithium blocks excess emotion but as human happiness and sadness are part of the psyche it is questionable about how much of either can be considered normal.

As an aside, I will always remember a remark made by an attractive young woman, an ex-patient with manic depression. She sat next to me not speaking for nearly an hour consumed by emotion. Eventually she looked at me with brimming eyes and said she wanted to go on a longed-for holiday with relatives but was afraid to, in case she became 'too happy'; that is, it might trigger a manic attack. That is the real tragedy of this illness.

Common Side Effects of Drugs

New drugs are tested for effectiveness and safety as well as cost-effective manufacturing. Drug chemical structures are complex and it is impossible to eliminate all negative effects. Common side effects are:

- headaches
- drowsiness.
- dry mouth
- sleeplessness
- tremors
- dystonia – abnormal movements like pacing, tapping the feet
- tardive dyskinesia – tongue rolling, facial grimacing
- akathisia – restlessness, unable to sit or stand comfortably

As research into DNA and computer modelling develop, pharmaceutical companies will be able to design targeted drugs with fewer negative effects. At a recent lecture, a pharmacist said the utopic dream of drugs designed for individuals was at least 20 years away. As knowledge of human genes progresses this is now a real possibility (albeit it will prove a very expensive option).

Electro Convulsive Therapy (ECT)

From early in the history of mental a shock was believed to cure patients by literally jolting them out of their insanity. In the days of Bethlem Asylum some cruel practices were invented to 'spin' the brain into wellness. These included fast revolving drums and chairs and even immersing patients into ice cold water. One wonders if these practices had more to do with the sadism of the attendants rather than a genuine desire to heal.

In the 1930's doctors noticed that epileptic seizures produced improvements in patients with schizophrenia. Scientists came to the conclusion that passing an electric current through the brain would mimic a seizure in the same way. This treatment was named Electro Convulsive Therapy (ECT); basically a new tag on a very old idea.

Delivery of Electro Convulsive Therapy

A general anaesthetic and muscle relaxant are administered to the patient. This stops severe convulsions and physical injury during treatment. Early versions of the treatment did not have these precautions and archive film footage of ECT procedures show patients bodies arching and writhing as shocks were administered without anaesthetic.

Watch the film 'A Beautiful Mind' with Russell Crowe in a fine performance as Nobel prize-winner John Nash. Dr Nash suffered from schizophrenia at a time when no drug therapies were available. The film depicts early ECT in a very graphic way.

Electrodes (wires attached to pads) are placed on either side of the skull or sometimes to one side only. The electrodes deliver an electric current through the brain. A course of 6 - 12 treatments is given twice a week with each shock lasting around 30 seconds.

The variables which affect the outcome of the treatment are:

- placement of the electrodes

- type of the electrical stimulus
- frequency of treatment

Is ECT Effective?

Even medical people would not be able to describe how this treatment works and until the clinical trials (reported below) it was administered more out of desperation than on hard evidence for its effectiveness. I never saw one of the psychiatric trainees who administered this treatment try it out on themselves.

ECT has been used for treatment in:

- severe depression
- schizophrenia
- mania
- catatonia

Many people in the medical profession and mental health voluntary organisations are against the use of ECT. There is widespread belief it causes permanent brain damage. On the other side of the coin, patients report relief from symptoms of intractable illness for which there is no other effective treatment.

NICE Report on ECT

The National Institute for Clinical Excellence (NICE) is a Government body responsible for testing clinical effectiveness and safety of medical treatments. In 2002 they were asked to prepare a report on the effectiveness of ECT. They looked at its usage in:

- severe depressive illness
- catatonia
- severe mania
- response to the treatment

The report aimed to look at the following areas:

- effectiveness of ECT

- conditions;
  - o duration, number, dosage the setting;
  - o the building, age of the equipment
  - o training given to those administering
- costs of treatment against using drug therapy
- patient acceptability

NICE recommendations were that ECT should only be used in cases of severe symptoms **and** where patients had previously responded to the treatment. This decision was based on evidence that ECT could lead to short or long term memory loss and potential brain damage.

The NICE report was well received by the mental health charities MIND and Together (formerly MACA) who nevertheless felt NICE could have gone further and banned ECT where patients did not consent.

The Royal College of Psychiatrists went further in wanting to be able to detain patients who refused ECT when clinicians felt it necessary for patient welfare. They challenged NICE in February 2003 asking for the ban on treating patients with severe symptoms to be removed. The appeal was dismissed.

Psychosurgery

You read earlier about Phineas Gage the Victorian railroad worker whose accident sparked off research into psychosurgery (surgery to the brain). This invasive and irreversible surgery was controversial from its beginnings even among psychiatrists who felt it unethical to interfere with personality through surgery.

Modern brain surgeons target microscopic areas of the brain with electrodes, aiming to disrupt or destroy cells where there are problems such as hyper-active brain cells. This process is called lesioning.

Although it appears some of these operations are successful in treating obsessive compulsive disorder (OCD) and severe depressive illness there is still no evidence on long-term effects. About a third of patients thus treated recover but the risks are strokes, seizures (sometimes developing years after the operation) and permanent brain damage. All such operations remain irreversible.

Battery Operated Brain Pacemaker Pack

Trials on a new intervention appear promising. The battery-operated Activa DBS (deep brain stimulation) device from Medicare is being used to relieve tremors in Parkinson's disease.

DBS is a sort of brain pacemaker. The device has proved so successful in the USA that many patients can purchase them through medical insurance. A computer is used for pinpointing the target area and electrodes are inserted whilst the patient is awake. When the current is turned on the patient can comment on its effects as the clinician varies the current.

According to the reports, patients can experience very rapid changes of mood. Amongst the known side effects are fatigue and an increase in weight. Although the pack must be replaced under anaesthetic patients have control over how much current is delivered once the pack is in place. The process **is** reversible. If successful this device might replace lesioning in years to come.

So much for the medical treatments. Let's turn now to some non medical alternatives.

Non Medical Models

"Who am I... if I like being that person, I'll come up. If not I'll stay down here until I'm somebody else"
Alice in Wonderland, Lewis Carroll

Chapter 8

A History of 'Talking Cures'

Contents of This Chapter:

A Brief History of Talking Cures
* Neurotic Mind & Hypnosis
* Jean Charcot [1835 - 1893] & Joseph Breuer [1842 - 1925]
* Sigmund Freud [1856 1939]]
* Psychoanalysis
* Carl Jung [1875 - 1961] - Analytical Psychology
    * Archetypes
    * New Thoughts about The Hero Archetype
    * Introverts and Extrovert Personalities.
    * The Spiritual Dimension of Personality
Mental Problems As 'Learned Behaviour'
* Pavlov [1849 -1936], Skinner [1904 - 1990] & Watson [1878-1958]
* Token Economy
* Encounter Groups
* Cognitive Therapy
* Cognitive Behavioural Therapy (CBT)
Post Jung: Other Stages Of Life
[The Elephant and the Three Blind Sages]
The Psychotherapists
Pioneering Work of Milton Erickson
Counselling
DBT
[The Story of Little Albert and The Pet Rat]

In this chapter I have grouped together a range of the so-called talking cures. I mentioned these briefly in my short history of mental illness. The term 'talking cure' was first used by one of Breuer's patients ('Anna O' - Bertha Pappenheim) to describe how she found relief from her symptoms by talking to Freud about her problems. There are many varieties of talking cure some more effective than others. Of course, the type I generally use called solution focussed or brief therapy is the best kind... All therapists will tell you that, so the best way to find out if you are in need of such therapy is to find someone you can trust. Easy really.

A Brief History of Talking Cures

Talking cure simply means that a patient/client speaks, writes, acts or otherwise communicates his difficulties to the therapist verbally. The roots of the talking cures are very ancient.

An early example is the Greek Delphic Oracle. A seeker with a problem would approach the pythoness or oracle and receive advice in return for goods or money. The Oracle went into a trance and predicted the seeker's future.

North American Indians held regular community meetings or pow-wows where troubled members of the community could talk about their problems. The whole community turned out to listen and offer advice. This was the forerunner of what is known as group therapy. There is rarely anything entirely new.

In later history, small villages all over the world had a wise person to whom people would go with their problems. These people were highly skilled in herbalism and healing. Simple country folk practising such remedies were regarded with awe and even jealousy. It was easy to accuse them of witchcraft and of blighting people and cattle. Indeed many thousands of innocent people were burned to death in the sixteenth century during the terror of the Pope's Spanish Inquisition.

Terry Pratchett makes an interesting observation in his amusing book 'Equal Rites' by referring to witchcraft as headology, or using common sense. Female wise women must have made the link between patient desire for a cure and the success of the treatment. Doctors refer to this phenomena as the placebo effect [or hope].

Conscious & Unconscious Mind

4) - output thinking [conscious]

We form conclusions about experiences from the products of 1, 2 & 3 - current sensory input, comparison with past experience AND collective unconscious or racial memories from our ancestry. This processing determines how the current event (experience) is viewed: (e.g. in negative or positive light; with fear; with joy; with outrage etc.)

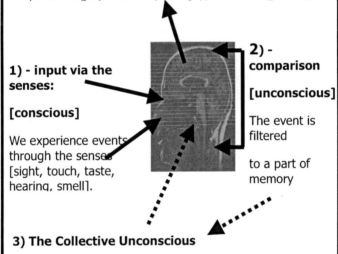

1) - input via the senses:

[conscious]

We experience events through the senses [sight, touch, taste, hearing, smell].

2) - comparison

[unconscious]

The event is filtered

to a part of memory

3) The Collective Unconscious

The part of mind apparent in dreams or feelings such as 'Deja vou' [sense of having experienced the same event on a previous occasion]. Jung's theory of ancient racial memories that contain the collective myths of our ancestors - 'collective unconscious'

Some modern scientists believe the mind is located throughout sensory cells in the body and is not limited to the area inside the brain.

Neurotic Mind & Hypnosis

Charcot [1835 - 1893] & Breuer [1842 - 1925]

Four major players responsible for spawning a large number of schools of psychotherapy and hypnotherapy, were Jean Martin Charcot and Joseph Breuer.

Charcot worked extensively with patients diagnosed with hysterical paralyses of limb or voice which are now referred to as conversion disorders. These were traumatic psychological incidents which became converted into physical paralyses. These types of disorder were common in the early eighteenth century.

Charcot discovered hypnotic suggestion would successfully free his patients from physical symptoms. Later, Breuer allowed his patients to talk under hypnosis and discovered this method freed them from neuroses.

Freud was a devotee of Charcot and Breuer and collaborated with them during his early career. Breuer and Freud named this hypnotic effect catharsis or cathexis, after the Greek word for cleansing or discharging.

Sigmund Freud [1856 1939]

Sigmund Freud and his follower Carl Jung were the founding fathers of psychological-based therapies. Freud was a follower of Breuer and became interested in uncovering hidden meanings in the mind which he hoped would allow patients to cathart (lose) all their neurotic symptoms. Although Freud used hypnosis a great deal early on, eventually he formed the view it was not the hypnotic state which cured his patients but the therapeutic relationship itself. He abandoned hypnosis in favour of treating patients in the conscious state. Freud developed a method he called psychoanalysis. Psyche is Greek for mind. He was attempting to understand what was happening in the subconscious mind.

Psychoanalysis

An analyst's job is to help their patients become aware of the unconscious mental processes. The patient is therefore able to understand their life difficulties and deal with problems more effectively. It is a long process as the analysand (an analyst's patient) has to struggle for self-understanding with very little verbal intervention from the analyst. Information will be gained from the patient from various means:

- **Expressed emotions** - the kind of emotions expressed when talking about specific subjects e.g. are they angry or happy when talking about specific things - parents, events, jobs. The emotion expressed will denote a negative or positive attitude toward the subject.
- **Free association of thoughts** - patients are allowed to free associate (talk freely without interruption). In doing so they reveal vital truths of which they are consciously unaware
- **Fantasies and dreams** – dreams are the mind's way of revealing facts or situations which the conscious mind rejects. Freud called them 'the royal road to the unconscious'.
- **Cathexis** - the process by which patients could lose (cathect) neuroses through understanding

A great deal is made of Freud's early theory that children repressed sexual interest in their parents (he called this the Oedipus complex after the mythological character Oedipus - see end of chapter). He believed children had hidden sexual desires for the opposite sex parent and this desire became repressed into a fantasy of rape.

Although three years later Freud changed his mind about this theory, many revile him as being responsible for a generation of sexually abused children who were further psychologically damaged through not being believed. However it cannot negate the valuable contribution to psychotherapeutic treatment.

Carl Jung [1875 - 1961] - Analytical Psychology

Carl Jung was a follower of Freud. Jung eventually split with Freud and became the founding father of modern analytical psychological theory. Jung's work was based on understanding the nature of the personality. He believed neurotic symptoms disappeared naturally in most people as the personality matured.

Jung believed everyone went through stages of development which peaked around mid life with the process of individuation, the stage of full integration of mind, body and spirit.

Archetypes

Jung was deeply interested in religion and philosophy. He looked at the common themes in many of the world's mythologies and deduced there was an unconscious link between the different story tellers because many characters and stories re-occurred in myths across the world. An example is the hero; a man born of a virgin, killed, resurrected then comes back to save his people.

Jung proposed that the personality contained archetypes such as the Wise Old Man, Trickster, Shadow, Mother. Analysing these archetypes (or sub personalities) was a means of integrating the personality according to Jung.

He also proposed the existence of a collective unconscious, a set of ancient racial memories which reside in the unconscious mind and can be accessed by analysing dreams.

New Thoughts about the Hero Archetype

In this age of so-called 'new man' therapists are questioning and updating the hero archetype. The hero also exists in women but is generally taken to be a male characteristic. You can read about this in Peter Tatham's book which I have listed in the further information section.

Introverts and Extrovert Personalities

Jung coined the terms introvert and extrovert to describe two different aspects of personality; the first inner and reflective, the latter more worldly and sociable.

Dream Interpretation

Jung believed that problems in the unconscious mind would be reflected in dreams which he called 'the royal road to the unconscious'. Dream interpretation became one of the tools of Jungian analysts who helped patients understand what dreams were revealing about their everyday life. This is a fascinating subject and I urge you to read further.

The Spiritual Dimension of Personality

Jung was fascinated by the beliefs of the Pueblo Indian tribe and studied them extensively. The Pueblo's believed that the sun rose every morning because of their daily rituals and without these the whole world would be plunged into darkness. Believing they were a vital aspect of existence gave the Pueblos a strong inner confidence and serenity which permeated their everyday lives.

This is from Jung's book 'Memories, Dreams and Reflections': 'when people feel they are living the symbolic life, that they are actors in the divine drama that gives the only meaning to human life.' This would be echoed by therapists who treat patients diagnosed with depressive illness.

Something wider than oneself that imbues life with meaning and colour and a place in the world are widely considered pre-requisites to a happy and fulfilled life. Jung inspired generations of psychotherapists with his inspired thinking and many of his discoveries are still in common usage in the modern world of psychotherapy.

Post Jung

Now we can begin to understand the progress of man's thoughts about his own nature; from feeling at the mercy of natural forces to moral beings that hold responsibility for their own mental health. With these changes in belief came corresponding changes to the type of treatments being developed.

Mental Problems As 'Learned Behaviour'

Pavlov [1849 -1936], Skinner [1904 - 1990] & Watson [1878-1958]

A separate school of thought was being developed by the 1930's by Ivan Pavlov who conducted experiments on animal behaviour. Pavlov had a bell rung each time his experimental dogs were given food. Before long, they learned to salivate as soon as they heard the bell, before the food arrived. Pavlov proved that responses to a stimulus could be changed in animals.

Following on from this work, John Watson (not the Dr Watson of Conan Doyle's Sherlock Holmes!) started working on his theory that behaviour was not naturally inborn but was conditioned [changed] through life experience. The two main arguments of Pavlov and Watson are now commonly known as 'nature versus nurture'.

We will gloss over the rather unethical story of Little Albert and his pet rat (well, all right, I'll add it to the end of this chapter). Watson finally managed to prove that human behaviour does adapt to situations.

Edward Thorndike and later Burrus Skinner enhanced these early behavioural theories. Skinner continued Thorndike's work by placing rats in a maze. The rats were rewarded for going in the right direction or punished by electric shock for going the wrong way. He drew the conclusion that animals and humans learn through reward and punishment a method adopted by many unenlightened establishments to this day. Mental illnesses treated by early behavioural therapy included depressive illness, phobias and addictions to drugs and alcohol.

Token Economy

Another form of behavioural therapy, in vogue in the 1970's, was token economy. Patients were rewarded for good behaviour by being given plastic tokens which they could exchange for cigarettes and extra cups of tea. What the psychologists on my Ward might not have been wise to was the illegal trade in tokens which went on after they left the ward... This shows that therapeutic regimes are not easy to implement when human cunning is involved!

Encounter Groups

Encounter groups were developed by Carl Rogers with the aim of improving human potential. Group members were encouraged to openly discuss their feelings with other members. These groups later became infamous for the potential to cause psychological damage through less than careful group leaders.

A friend of mine attended one of these groups. The group philosophy was to create immunity to problems by ridiculing or making light of sad experiences.

My friend was in tears as she described the suicide of her friend whilst group members taunted her with distasteful remarks I shall not repeat here. Her final words on the subject were that she could not wait to have her turn to have a go, because she felt so traumatised herself. This sort of group behaviour seemed to promote bullying rather than genuine healing. This therapy has now been discredited.

Cognitive Therapy

Later, psychologists realized that a purely behavioural view was too narrow. Cognitive (cognitive = to recognise) therapists came to believe that people who consistently experienced frustrations, anxieties and emotional problems have faulty ways of thinking. They attributed part of the blame for these negative patterns to dysfunctional childhood but the other side being negative experiences in everyday life.

By recognising, challenging and changing faulty thinking patterns the negative emotions and behaviours connected with them could be replaced by positive ones. This is the basis of cognitive therapy.

Cognitive Behavioural Therapy (CBT)

Later still psychologists (these people seem to come out of the woodwork) developed a theory combining behaviourism with cognitive therapy into (guess what) cognitive-behavioural therapy. This is currently a treatment of choice for emotional disorders, recommended by the National Institute for Clinical Excellence [NICE].

Post Jung: Other Stages of Life

Primitive cultures virtually ran on rituals or rites of passage. These were taken seriously as powerful acts of magic which ensured survival of the tribe, safe passage to the next stage of life or through the underworld after death. There are many examples;

- American Indian rain dances
- Egyptian mummification and death rituals
- stone age burial rites

Religious ceremonies reflect some of these ancient rites of birth, puberty and death;

- Christian christenings
- Jewish ceremonies of coming of age - Bar Mitzvah
- Hindu cremations at the burning ghats
- Buddhists death rites - the towers of silence

In Western and other modern societies people no longer believe in essential magic (such as the Pueblo's beliefs about the sun) but still mark the passage of time in the development of an individual by performing certain rites. For example, dressing up, eating particular foodstuffs [e.g. wedding cake, birthday cakes], drinking a larger amount of alcohol and receiving congratulatory cards (marriages, coming of age and birthdays respectively).

Some psychotherapists view these age-related rituals as symbolic of the vital stages which must be successfully negotiated so that the psyche (mind) develops properly.

Some people get stuck in a particular stage of life. For example, have you ever met an eternal youth (puer eternis), a mature man who acts like an adolescent; or a young woman who clings to the security of childhood by acting in a child-like manner? The latter is sometimes seen as responsible for the development of eating disorders (anorexia or bulimia). In a fragile and dangerous world this need for security is understandable and poignant. This system of thinking is known as the 'stages of life' theory.

Theorists (people who develop ideas) who follow the stages-of-life method might recommend therapeutic communities or work-based therapies (skills training for jobs combined with therapy) to their patients. In these places, they can learn the correct behaviours which will enable them to successfully negotiate their current life stage, before moving on to the next.

The Elephant & the Three Blind Sages

Before I describe some of the work of the psychotherapists, there is an object lesson. Many therapists are evangelistic about their particular school of thought (theory) and claim to have hit upon the only workable therapy. This is certain to be untrue because of the diversity of human nature.

So, before you dive into a particular cause or decide to train or to go into therapy, consider my version of this Taoist tale.

Three blind sages (wise men) came across an animal in the forest which blocked their path. In order to find out what manner of creature it was, they decided to feel it. The first sage said the animal was long and thin like a snake (he found the tail). The second said it reminded him of a pillar (he found a foot). The third sage said that the creature was huge and reached the sky (he found the base of its huge side).

The Psychotherapists

Freud and Jung were followed by a whole raft of individual psychotherapists trying to make their names by developing their own pet theory. All these were concerned with states of mind or psyche. Psyche is a Greek word meaning mind (and also the name of a Greek goddess). Psychotherapy merely means therapy of the mind.

Pioneering Work by Milton Erickson

You may think that by now all the possibilities about different kinds of therapies would have been explored, but no. Theorists are good at finding jobs for themselves!

Solution focussed or brief interventions are similar. If you want to go into all the subtleties I suggest you read one of the many books on the subject. Although many people claim to have invented brief therapy the real 'Father' was Milton Erickson.

In the 1970's Erickson (an American Psychiatrist) pioneered a quirky method which rapidly had patients flocking to his clinics.

As part of his attempts to learn to walk again after being confined to a wheelchair because of polio, he had closely observed visitors, family and people passing by, noting their behaviour traits and especially how babies learned to walk. He became expert at observing how people did things and how they approached life (what he called people's 'map of the world'.)

After years of observation, Erickson decided that everyone already had within their unconscious minds the key to resolving their own problems. The work of the therapist was to help them utilise these strategies for their current problems.

Erickson initially advocated a kind of auto-hypnosis whereby the patient, in a very relaxed state, could imagine themselves free of their problem and describe how life would be without it. From that starting point, Erickson would set patients tasks designed to enhance the healing effect.

Many people mistakenly believe that Erickson = hypnosis. But, that is a fallacy, as that was only a small part of his work. He learned to talk to patients using their own symbolic language or metaphors. The crux of his method was establishing the meaning of the problem from the patient's point of view. This point is often lost, especially if you read some of the 'teaching tales', which today seem outlandish and often bizarre.

However, remember that any pioneering work seems far less sophisticated when compared with later developments; think of early computers, animations such as 'Hitchhikers Guide to the Galaxy' or even some of the early treatments for mental illness I have already described to you – electric eels for example!

By empathising in this way, Erickson was utilising the placebo effect, a process which is well known to medical people. Placebo can be considered the hope or expectation factor; when you think lucky you will be lucky as Evadne Price (the palmist) used to say.

Solution therapies are fast, cheap, effective and therefore subject to ridicule by non enlightened analytical therapists. However, they are approved by NICE (I am pleased to say) and rapidly becoming treatment of choice within the cash-strapped NHS.

Patients like this style of treatment because it is not invasive and does not involve painful analytical resurrection of life history. It does not work in all cases and there is room in the therapy world for many kinds of treatment. A newer version of this therapy is known as motivational interviewing.

Counselling

Counselling is a relatively new kind of therapy and brings us right up to date with the talking therapies. Some schools favour individual counselling, others within groups; some believe the dynamic of the relationship is paramount, whilst other feel that social interaction is the only way of maintaining mental health. Some schools use problem solving whilst analytical types seek insight as a key to change. Remember the elephant.

DBT

And finally, because you must be ready for a break. Dialectical behaviour therapy (DBT) has been developed by American Psychologist Marsha Lineham for patients with personality disorders. Dialectical means at either end. The name reflects both ends of the high emotional states experienced by people with personality disorders. Such people become either over-emotional (in order to be heard by a non-listening parent) or else hide their feelings (in order to be accepted by a critical parent).

DBT aims to pull the two extremes together so the patient learns neither to hide nor overtly express feelings but make themselves more reasonably understood; or become less critical of others and at the same time less critical towards themselves.

In DBT the relationship between therapist and patient has to be cooperative as they are dealing with the very delicate area of the patient's belief system. DBT develops positive behaviours in individual situations, promotes self understanding and offers reward in the form of praise. It aims to build on individual successes to spread change through the chain of unproductive behaviours.

&&&&&&&&&&&&&&&&&&&&&&&&&&

The Story of Little Albert and the Pet Rat

I did promise to present the story of Arthur and the pet rat. Behaviour therapists will hate me for relaying this but what the heck - live dangerously if you live at all!

The story goes, Watson was seeking to prove that Pavlov's theory worked with humans as well as animals. That is, humans could be conditioned (taught) to behave in a certain way.

In an experiment which would be frowned upon today, they found a boy called Little Albert who had a pet white rat which he was very fond of.

As the boy started playing with his pet Watson made loud noises just behind the boy, who was naturally startled. After doing this a many times, Albert became distressed whenever his pet appeared.

So Watson was able to conclude from this dubious research that anyone can be induced to react in a different way when they are conditioned to do so. And perhaps how ruthless psychologists are when pursuing research.

History does not record reactions from Little Albert's parents.

Say not, 'I have found the truth', but rather, 'I have found a truth' .. for the soul walks upon all paths.
Khalil Gibran

Chapter 9

'Alternatives':
Holistic, Green & Ecological

This Chapter includes:

Art Therapies
* Art Therapy
* Music therapy
* Psychodrama
Visualisation
* Affirmations
Hands-on Therapies
* Aromatherapy
* Healing & Reiki
* Laying-on of Hands
* Reflexology
Homeopathy
Green therapies
* books on prescription
* pets on prescription
* gym & green gym

Spiritual Therapies
* Humour Therapy
* Taoism & Buddhism
* Mindfulness
* Yoga
Traditional Chinese Medicine
* Herbal Medicine
* Acupuncture
* Massage - Shiatsu
* Tai Chi and Qi Gong
Ecological therapies
Exercising Caution
* Healing Objects
* Good Practitioners
Research into Complementaries
Summing Up

There are hundreds of complementary therapies from the almost-accepted by the medical profession to the downright dubious. I found it difficult to decide what to include without making this chapter so long it would bankrupt the publisher so I hope you find this selection interesting.

My favourite is Dr Hunter Patch Adams 'Gesundheit Institute' to which traditional medical practitioners are flocking. Watch the movie 'Patch Adams' if you can which is the often hilarious but poignant story of Dr Adams controversial humour therapy clinic.

The terms complementary and alternative are used indiscriminately but a rule of thumb is that if a therapy claims to be alternative the therapists are probably claiming their treatment works independently, rather than as an adjunct to medicine. If in doubt take a rain check with a trusted doctor who is interested in other forms of treatment.

Holistic practitioners hold the view there is a strong link between mind, body and spirit and treat all three. Imagine you have a cold; does it affect how you feel and think? If you are well and the sun is shining, does that affect your mental state? Refer to the diagram 'man as a holistic being'.

Mind relationships, suitable occupation, self-identity, ability to relax

Body physical health; the best an individual achieves regardless of disabilities

Spirit perception of beauty, the arts, spiritual & religious experience

Holism is borne out in the experiences of contemporary and historical figures who carved out meaningful lives despite profoundly difficult mental, physical or spiritual conditions. I am sure you can think of many examples but this is a short list of those who fascinate me:

- **Helen Keller** – born blind, deaf and dumb; became a writer and teacher
- **Anne Frank** - young Jewish diarist who died in a concentration camp
- **Richard Dadd** - Victorian artist who lived most of his life in Bethlem Asylum
- **Viktor Frankl** - Psychiatrist & writer who survived Auschwitz but committed suicide in his later years
- **W.H. Davies** - the celebrated poet & writer who lived as a tramp until 'discovered' by George Bernard Shaw

Art Therapies

Originally considered somewhat fringe, art therapies are now offered in progressive psychiatric hospitals, prisons, care homes and other areas where people are likely to benefit from freedom of creative expression. Art used as therapy has an interpretive element. However, writing, drawing and reading are excellent methods for de-stressing whether or not they are a part of some formal therapy scheme.

Art therapies are particularly useful for people who find it hard to express feelings or ideas verbally. There are considerable benefits over talking therapy in that:

- they allow freedom of expression - does not depend on the direction selected by a therapist
- they can be a symbolic vehicle for therapy
- art is potentially less threatening than talking therapy
- an infinite number of possibilities can be created and explored

This is a relatively new field in a formal sense but if you think about art on a symbolic level, mankind has used such expressions for thousands of years through all cultures for beautification, ritualistic purposes and entertainment:

- **cave paintings** - graceful images of men and animals, the drawings linked to magic - to ensure the success of the hunt, perhaps a way of keeping the people safe

- **religious art** - Russian icons; wall paintings of Christian themes; symbolic patterns in Islamic art; the colourful paintings and sculptures of Hindu culture

- **ritualistic music/dance** - tribal music and dance for ceremonial purposes; rain dances of the American Indians; sema - the whirling ecstatic religious dance of the Dervishes; classical symbolic Indian dance interpreting stories from Hindu mythology

- **drama** - Japanese Kabuki and masked No theatrical

performances which depict the major events of human life - battles, love, moral conflicts; early English dumb-show pantomime as performed by John Rich; the Christian cycle of passion plays of Oberammergau

A very brief overview follows but do read further on this subject.

Art Therapy

Patients are given media (crayon, paint, chalk) with which to draw or paint. The aim is to develop the patient's interest in what they have created. The therapist discusses the meaning and symbolism of the finished piece for example the forms, shapes, colours and imagery.

During therapy the patient has the opportunity to develop and change their original concept and therefore their outlook on the original content. Art is said to be particularly valuable for patients with little sense of self esteem or few other means of self expression.

Music therapy

Music therapy is used to motivate, support in emotional crises, reduce stress, enhance creativity and achieve identity within a culture. It helps patients who feel little sense of belonging.

In reminiscence therapy for elderly people, music evocative of their period in history lessens the sense of isolation and revives memories of community and a sense of belonging that are so vital to mental health.

Patients with emotional or neurotic disorders are asked to listen to music which reflects their mood. Gradually, through their knowledge of music, the therapist provides music which leads the patient out of a negative mood into a more positive state of mind.

Psychodrama

Psychodrama helps patients relive life events through role play. The therapist might exchange roles or mirror (copy) the patient's behaviour in order to help the patient understand what is happening to them in the real life situation. Interpretations or alternative endings for the same sequence of events are explored in intense but enlightening sessions within a safe environment.

There is no audience for individual drama therapy but there is a group version where groups of patients enact different archetypal scenes, for example a family outing, wedding or funeral.

Visualisation Techniques

These are not art therapies in the strict sense but I have included them in this section as they are used in psychotherapy. I am keen on using these techniques which are natural, easily taught and can be used by an individual to:

- promote relaxation and freedom from stress
- diffuse anger and negative thinking
- encourage goals and wishes for the future
- improve relationships and performance
- help problem solving

When you daydream or mentally revise for an exam or think about someone before meeting them you are conjuring up an image of what you want to happen in the future. This is visualisation. It is our means of making a daydream into reality. This is what cave art is all about. Everything we create in the real world starts with an idea (a powerful thought).

Extravagant claims are sometimes made about creating great wealth without effort or curing terminal illness which give visualisation an unrealistic image.

The techniques are more easily learned with the encouragement of a therapist but using guided imagery CDs or tapes work well.

Affirmations

Where visualisation takes the form of a brief saying or collection of sayings these are called affirmations. Affirmations are used not only therapeutically but also in religious settings as mental reinforcers of faith, for example the Christian Nicene Creed, the Muslim cry 'Allah Akbar' (God is great). Even war cries and football chants are affirmations of a sort as they seek to unite, whip up an encouraging atmosphere and mobilise action.

Affirmations are sometimes used in a negative way, as a form of brainwashing and for stirring up hatred; calls-to-arms for so-called 'holy' wars; well-rehearsed one-liners by totalitarian state leaders; ways of controlling the emotion of crowds and mobs.

George Orwell's book '1984' contains a good example of an affirmation. The message 'big brother is watching you' is played continuously on public address systems over portraits of the dictator to remind citizens of his power. One liner affirmations are used widely in TV advertising and in printed matter as 'strap lines' (slogans).

Hands-on Therapies

There are many physical therapies mostly derived from ancient techniques. Physical therapies involve touching the patient to promote calm and a sense of well being. Our forbears were highly preoccupied with health and appearance; between farming and making war that is.

Massage has been known for thousands of years as a way of relieving muscular and mental stress. Mark Anthony is said to have enjoyed massaging Cleopatra's feet during dinner parties much to the disgust of the Emperor Octavian. Shiatsu appears with the Chinese therapies in case you wonder why it does not appear here.

Aromatherapy

Aromatherapy is an ancient therapy. This is a body massage using scented oils derived from plants. Massage is a pleasant way of unwinding and the perfume from the oils adds to the delightful experience of an aromatherapy massage. There is no real evidence that it is any more effective than a good holiday or a massage without herbs. It is a question of preference.

Practitioners use a variety of herbs and plants known for their pleasant aromas. Some of these plant materials are used as medicines. I am not aware of any research in this area but, as I've said before, there is a lack of funding for research and much of this is currently spent on drug therapies. The rule must be as always, if it works for you then go for it but don't spend great wads of money before sampling it.

Healing & Reiki

Healing is based on the belief that an energy circulates the body. The Chinese call it chi, the Hindus prana, the Japanese ki. We all have the ability to move this energy but some are more gifted.

Some practitioners link healing to faith but this is not prerequisite to giving or receiving healing. I remember trying to join a healing circle for training. I was asked by the leader if I accepted Christ was the son of God. When I replied that I did not I was excluded from the circle. Narrow mindedness is not a helpful trait for a healer. Anyone can be a healer if they care to develop this simple folk cure.

Laying-on of Hands

Healing is performed by the laying-on of hands or placing the hands on the patient's head or shoulders. The patient should feel the heat of the healer's hands. The contact itself is often enough to give comfort to a distressed person.

Reiki is healing by moving the hands around the patient's body without touching. This is useful for people who don't like being touched for example autistic people like myself. There are no herbs or medicines involved. Reiki can be learned in a group setting by anyone with the inclination. The key to a really good therapist is their degree of sensitivity and sincerity.

Reflexology

Reflexology or foot massage is ancient and was practised during early Egyptian times. There are carvings of practitioners giving what appears to be a foot massage in the tomb of the Physician in Saqqara, Egypt although some archaeologists do interpret these treatments as being manicures or pedicures. The principle behind reflexology is similar to that of acupuncture. The Chinese and some other cultures believe there are meridians or lines of energy running down the body from the head to the hands and through the trunk to the feet. When pressure is applied to a finger or toe it increases the energy flow in the organs along that meridian line and promotes healing. This therapy is amongst the first I tried as a trainee. My first student patient had a back problem. At my first probing, much to my horror, she shot out of her chair like a startled rabbit. She pronounced to the class that she felt a spurt of energy up her spine and went around praising my healing ability which also had the beneficial effect of massaging my ego and giving me great kudos in the class. Probably as well that no one was not around to see if the effect lasted!

Homeopathy

Homeopathy although favoured by the royal family remains a controversial therapy. Its modern form was invented by Samuel Hahnemann at a time when blood letting with leeches and purgatives were common treatments. Homeopathy might well have had the edge under those circumstances. Homeopathists treat disease with medicines which mimic the effects of the disease. They believe only a very tiny amount of the original medicinal herb is required and the dilution is so small there is very little of the preparation left in the base carrier. The carrier is the water or alcohol in which the herb is distilled.

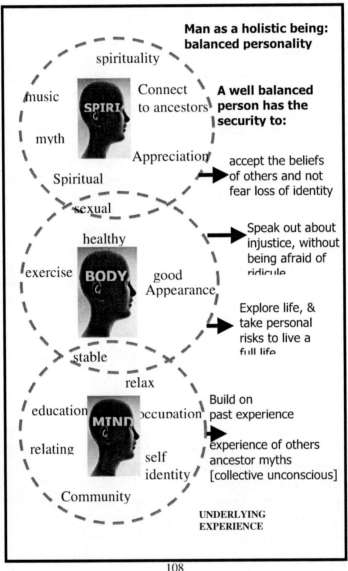

Man as a holistic being: balanced personality

spirituality

Connect to ancestors

music

myth

Appreciation

Spiritual

sexual

healthy

exercise

good Appearance

stable

relax

education

occupation

relating

self identity

Community

A well balanced person has the security to:

accept the beliefs of others and not fear loss of identity

Speak out about injustice, without being afraid of ridicule

Explore life, & take personal risks to live a full life

Build on past experience

experience of others ancestor myths [collective unconscious]

UNDERLYING EXPERIENCE

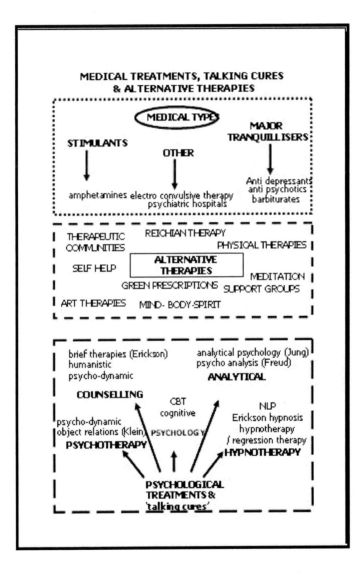

MEDICAL TREATMENTS, TALKING CURES & ALTERNATIVE THERAPIES

MEDICAL TYPES

STIMULANTS

OTHER

MAJOR TRANQUILLISERS

amphetamines

electro convulsive therapy
psychiatric hospitals

Anti depressants
anti psychotics
barbiturates

THERAPEUTIC COMMUNITIES

REICHIAN THERAPY

PHYSICAL THERAPIES

SELF HELP

ALTERNATIVE THERAPIES

GREEN PRESCRIPTIONS

MEDITATION

SUPPORT GROUPS

ART THERAPIES

MIND- BODY-SPIRIT

brief therapies (Erickson)
humanistic
psycho-dynamic

analytical psychology (Jung)
psycho analysis (Freud)

ANALYTICAL

COUNSELLING

CBT
cognitive

NLP
Erickson hypnosis
hypnotherapy
/ regression therapy

psycho-dynamic
object relations (Klein)

PSYCHOLOGY

PSYCHOTHERAPY

HYPNOTHERAPY

**PSYCHOLOGICAL TREATMENTS &
'talking cures'**

There is anecdotal evidence this system works and many people swear by these. But beware spending a lot of money unless you are sure it works for you because these are very expensive.

Green Prescriptions

Green prescriptions are a relatively new alternative to traditional drug medications, specifically for anxiety conditions or mild depressive illness. NICE guidelines direct that self help or psycho-education (education about the mind) is first treatment of choice. There are many kinds so I will content myself to describe three - books, pets and gym.

Books

Patients do not have to belong to a library in order to get a book on prescription (or bibliotherapy to give it its posh name). The books are selected and reviewed in advance by the clinicians and librarians, are on various topics including:

- assertiveness
- anxiety
- depression
- self esteem

Each practitioner has a pad of prescriptions with the book titles written on them and prescribes after agreeing with the patient on a suitable subject. This is a new tack on an old idea, if you think about books such as the Bible, Koran or any religious tract which for thousands of years brought comfort and healing to readers.

It is easier to recommend books pre-vetted by therapists because there are so many on the market. This is one prescription you can dispense for yourself by browsing the local library, second-hand bookshop or online. Tip of the day: I tend to borrow books from the library first before purchasing ones I really like.

Pets

Pets on prescription? Yes it does sound an odd idea, and you will not find many on offer yet. Basically, there is evidence that owning a pet is calming and reduces loneliness.

Lewisham Primary Care Trust are conducting a small trial whereby GP's can prescribe a dog to a patient whom they feel might benefit and therefore reduce the amount of money being spent on drugs and invasive surgery. Those with heart problems, diabetes and blood pressure might be good candidates. An amount of money is offered (to pay for the animal, its feed and vet bills) rather than an animal itself in case you have visions of a mini zoo in the surgery backyard.

The idea of pets as therapy is not new. The organisation Pets as Therapy (PAT) has been operating since 1983 with registered animals (dogs and cats) and their owners visiting all kinds of establishments including hospitals, care homes and hospices. I have appended their web address in the index. However, pets on prescription goes one stage further by offering pet ownership.

Those who cry 'waste of resources' should look further into the scheme. Economically, considering the cost to the NHS of heart surgery and mental illness brought on by stress is huge. This needs to be taken into consideration against initial set up costs.

Gym & Green Gym

Exercise is known to be beneficial to mental health. A fairly recent scheme allows discounts for membership of gymnasiums for people with mental health problems. Again, this is sparse so don't expect to find these schemes everywhere. This system fits well as part of a national campaign for healthier communities. And a nice little earner for leisure centres.

Green gym is slightly different in being a practical way of improving the environment as well as getting healthy (and free) outdoor exercise. The schemes are run locally by volunteers in conjunction with organisations such as the National Trust and Local Authorities. Projects depend upon negotiations between green gym group leaders and the organisation involved.

Green Gyms are primarily concerned with practical outdoor tasks which offer exercise for participants at the same time (not as they say 'cheap labour'). Some examples of projects include: tree planting, building nature areas for schools, dry stone walling.

This seems an excellent scheme all round for those interested in improving communities and their own health. There is a web address in the index.

Spiritual Therapies

Humour Therapy

Medical practitioners are flocking to the USA to work with Dr Hunter Patch Adams (doctor and clown) at the Gesundheit Institute, where laughter and creativity are the medicines on offer.

The film 'Patch Adams' movingly demonstrates the reasons behind his belief in humour to relieve illness. Humour is known to release natural pain relievers called endorphins into the body and decrease the hormones responsible for stress. And laughter is at least free.

Taoism & Buddhism

Taoism or Buddhism are not the dry complex philosophies which you might expect and come complete with physical and spiritual exercises for attaining peace of mind and a healthy body.

Taoism (The Way') and Buddhism are spiritual ways of living rather than religious organisations. Taoism needs to be experienced in simple ways rather than by studying texts.

Buddhism for lay people is practised through meditation; training the mind to be still and to concentrate. It is not necessary to have a belief in the faith of Taoism or Buddhism in order to benefit from the spiritual practice of meditation.

Mindfulness

In his book 'The Miracle of Mindfulness' Thich Nhat Hanh (pronounced Titch Nat Han) advocates simple daily practices which will bring tranquillity into your daily life. Taoists are renowned for their peaceful demeanour and sense of humour. Mindfulness is a particular kind of meditation.

Mindfulness works by allowing the mind to become tranquil and accept what is happening 'right now' without judging, worrying or trying to change things. The practice is simply narrowing the concentration to one small area of activity. You can practice mindfulness whatever you are doing; washing up, watching a candle flame, walking or shopping. You don't need special clothes, expensive objects or a special place to practice.

Its simplicity is sometimes difficult for Westerners to accept as we are used to dealing with multiple sensory inputs; noises, sounds, smells and the rush and activity of everyday living.

Mindfulness has been integrated into treatment for depressive illness and all kinds of stress conditions. It is being used within the NHS particularly in cancer care.

Yoga

Yoga in the Western world is a watered-down version of the incredible physical and mental exercises practised by Yogis (holy men) in India. Yoga promotes physical strength, suppleness and mental health. It is practised extensively within prisons as a way of allowing inmates and prison warders to relax and experience spiritual freedom. The governing body in the UK for this discipline is the Wheel of Yoga.

Some yoga postures are complex and require a great deal of stamina but beginners are trained in simpler versions. There is a form called hatha yoga in which practitioners concentrate on breathing techniques.

Traditional Chinese Medicine

An ancient system of healing, Chinese medicine incorporates many elements designed to keep the energies (chi) flowing and the patient healthy. It balances the two opposites of yin and yang which are present in every living being (e.g. cold and hot, light and dark), and the five elements (water, wood, fire, earth, and metal) each of which are related to a season (the 5th season is called late summer).

Unlike Western medicine which is based on treatment for existing symptoms, the Chinese doctor's job is to prevent his patients from getting ill. They are paid when their patients are well but not when they are ill. This seems an excellent means of paying UK dentists.

The practice consists of several disciplines such as herbal medicine, acupuncture, massage therapy and tai chi or qi gong (the latter two are soft martial arts).

Herbal Medicine

The Chinese herbal has been in existence since the 3rd century AD. Chinese add to existing knowledge rather than superseding old ways with new as in Western culture. Chi energy is balanced using a combination of plant materials for instance bark, flowers, leaves and roots, even poisonous material. Some are made into pills and some are dried and presented to the patient to be boiled with water as a decoction or eaten. Do not expect the dried herbs to taste nice or you will be disappointed.

The system is not meant to cure individual illness or conditions but to re-balance and vitalise the whole body. The body's energy consists of three elements:

- chi - energy or lifeforce (heart and lungs)
- chen - spirit (happiness and mental alertness)
- jing - personal potential for growth

Acupuncture

Acupuncture works in a similar way to reflexology except that needles are used to puncture the skin along meridian lines of energy. Sometimes practitioners use moxibustion or bundles of burning herbs instead of needles. There is much evidence of the effectiveness of this therapy both for physical complaints and stress disorders. During a recent BBC programme on alternative medicine (mentioned several times now!) it was found that when the doctor was pushing needles deep into the skin an MRI scan could detect nerve pain centres being affected. Proof this does actually work.

Massage - Shiatsu

Shiatsu is Japanese but I put it in this section as it works along the same lines as Chinese medicine. Shiatsu means healing with the fingers and is a form of massage using pressure with the aim of balancing the bodily energy or ki. It is similar to acupuncture in that it is designed to restore the body to equilibrium and wholeness. Unlike Western massage the patient lies on the floor on a blanket or mat to receive the massage.

Tai Chi and Qi Gong

You may have seen tai chi beautifully performed during the current programme breaks on BBC television by a group of young people dressed in red or films of older Chinese people exercising in public parks. Beautiful and dancelike in form, the main benefits are achieved when the exercises are performed slowly. These are soft martial arts whereas karate and such like are known as the hard martial arts.

Having tried tai chi it is much harder than it looks. You have to concentrate hard whilst learning to balance as you move infinitely slowly. The elegance of Masters comes with years of practice.

Chi and Qi Gong are ways of strengthening the inner organs of the body, promoting suppleness, dexterity and inducing relaxation. They are highly recommended for promoting calm.

Masters of the art are able to perform feats like throwing students or groups of students off balance using light and deft movements utilising the students' own chi energy against them. I have seen this done and it is quite remarkable.

Ecological Therapies

Eco therapies connect people with their environment. I have already mentioned one kind of eco therapy which is green gym.

Rock climbing and walking groups have been found to be successful in anxiety reduction, offering companionship, increasing personal confidence and team spirit. All of these impact on mental health. If you are cynical about eco therapy try watching 'Brat Camp' (Channel 4, 9pm Wednesdays currently).

As you can see, the stodgy NHS is starting to come away from the old idea of autocratic doctors dispensing pills towards a wider vision of mental health and well-being. Like other new regimes, this will obviously encourage a variety of responses from the public:

☹ ridicule (cynics)
☹ frivolous and money wasting (traditionalists)
☺ praise (green and ecological campaigners)
☺ interest (researchers into effective remedies for mental health)

Exercising Caution

Professor Sykes (by now she must owe me royalties..) saw much evidence of the effectiveness of healing and arts like acupuncture but concluded it was not particularly what the healer did or used but the relationship between healer and patient. And, of course, the belief of the patient in a successful outcome (hope or placebo effect).

Healing Objects

Do be careful when offered expensive doo-dads, potions, rocks, coloured waters etc. for sale as therapeutic objects, unless you have a very strong feeling about their effectiveness (i.e. don't buy them out of desperation for an instant cure.). Albeit miracles happen, it is in the nature of miracles to be extremely rare.

Ask yourself if the same cure can be had by looking at attractive landscapes, natural colours and forms or even watching a naughty movie; all relatively cheap or free of charge. A nice view, trinket or book will aid hands-on healing by someone trustworthy.

The mind has an amazing natural power to assimilate beauty, tranquillity, colour and positive emotions which are very healing.

Good Practitioners

There are many charlatans in this highly profitable business area. People who are weary, stressed or discomforted are easily duped and it is natural for human beings to want instant relief from life's problems. Don't expect memberships of seemingly august bodies to be the only factor. Judge by your instincts too.

Research into Complementary Medicines

Sadly few areas of complementary medicines have been properly researched due to lack of funding and probably lack of interest by the medical profession. Indeed any kind of research is difficult as human beings are complex entities physically and psychologically and what works for one person cannot be guaranteed to work for another. Caveat emptor 'let the buyer beware'.

Summing Up Green Alternatives to Therapy

An interesting paper called 'the politics of happiness' (New Economics Foundation, NEF) is currently looking at the many facets of human happiness. Surprisingly, they discovered that modern society is starting to change its view that ever increasing ability to purchase electronic goodies results in happiness - far from it.

I think I will leave this section on alternatives to medication with a telling quotation from the above paper:

"the problem with late capitalism is not what it gives us - there is little wrong with Faberge or Furbys. It is what it is failing to give us: companionship, time for reflection, spirituality, security, intellectual development, and joy in our children. We have come so far, only to miss so much."

Social & Community Models of Care

"Arsonist .. served 21 years in jail.. The Judge wrote "In a just Society, he should not be in prison but in a secure place where he could receive treatment"
Local newspaper report

CHAPTER 10

Social Models of Care

This Chapter includes:
Social Interpretations
Care in the Community
• A Successful Resettlement
• Community Facilities
Therapeutic Communities
Rehabilitation Units

Social Interpretations

In some primitive tribes hallucinations are seen as possession by ancestor spirits. People who experience such hallucinations are revered rather than viewed as psychotic. In a reversal, Western psychiatrists have been accused of labelling West Indian patients as schizophrenic because they fail to recognise the cultural significance of possession by ghosts and spirits.

Modern social theorists believe mental illnesses are conditions caused by communication difficulties and that given love, support and understanding anyone will thrive. The psychiatrist R. D. Laing wrote extensively about the myth of mental illness following much the same theme.

Viktor Frankl, a Jewish Doctor imprisoned in Auschwitz, wrote that human beings can survive in atrocious conditions provided they find meaning in their lives. Frankl lived and worked as a psychiatrist for years after the war until his tragic suicide in 1997. He developed his ideas during his imprisonment in Auschwitz as a way of surviving his ordeal. He called his new therapy logotherapy (logos is Greek for meaning). The triangle of logotherapy is based on:

- **creativity** - what we give to the world
- **experiencing** - what we receive from the world
- **attitude** - how we perceive the world

I have given you the website details for logotherapy in the further information section because I believe Frankl's thinking is fundamental to 21st century attitudes toward mental health and healthy community living.

Care in the Community – the 1990's

I noticed a man from a nearby Group Home for mentally ill patients. He was standing on a street corner singing to himself and cradling a pile of incontinence pads. His face wore an expression of incredible sadness.

In the 1990's the Government passed the Community Care Act. This was the Government initiative to close Asylums and settle patients into the Community. Although the public were tolerant with mental patients who returned to their hospitals at night it was a different matter when ex-patients came to live within the community.

Many patients were fearful at the prospect of leaving their institutional homes after decades of having friends, the security of daily routine and laid-on purposeful activity.

Groups of three or four patients were allocated small houses called group homes. Others were moved to rented social housing in the form of bed-sits or small flats. Asylum buildings were sold to developers who often turned them into luxury homes and flats. Ironically the very places stigmatised by society thus became the sought-after homes of the middle classes. I noted with amusement that on one such development all reference to the former asylum had been removed from the place name. This is in marked contrast to other listed buildings where blue plaques celebrate the historic aspects.

Local Authorities failed to educate the public about mental illness and I am sure this is why re-settlement was not an overwhelming success. Many former patients were left to structure their own lives between infrequent visits by community workers. As well as coping with the symptoms of their mental illness they had to remember to take medication.

Ex patients were socially inexperienced and had limited income with little opportunity of paid work. It might be difficult for readers to appreciate how difficult life would be under these circumstances. Those who managed to thrive deserve recognition for their success.

A Successful Resettlement

One of my lasting memories is of an old man who had been taking ecclesiastical training when he became ill. This happened before the development of medication for schizophrenia.

Re-settled in a group home after spending most of his life in an Asylum he managed to find a concert hall a bus ride away. For the remainder of his days he enjoyed his weekly classical music concerts. I remember being seated behind him and asking someone near him the name of the composer of the piece being played. He turned and informed me with a beatific smile it was Massenet's Meditation and then added "my name is [xxx] and I live in a group home." The music was all he had left of his vocation. His sheer determination to travel several miles each week to attend these concerts in order to enjoy the music was, as the organiser later remarked to me, "a triumph".

Community Facilities

There were few community facilities at this time due to lack of funding also little legal backup to ensure criminal patients received treatment in prison.

After a spate of negative articles in the press about murderous attacks which people attributed to ex-patients, society began to

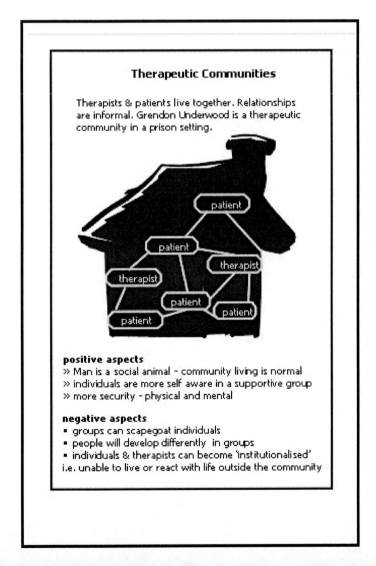

Therapeutic Communities

Therapists & patients live together. Relationships are informal. Grendon Underwood is a therapeutic community in a prison setting.

patient

patient

therapist

therapist

patient

patient

patient

positive aspects
>> Man is a social animal - community living is normal
>> individuals are more self aware in a supportive group
>> more security - physical and mental

negative aspects
• groups can scapegoat individuals
• people will develop differently in groups
• individuals & therapists can become 'institutionalised' i.e. unable to live or react with life outside the community

turn against mentally ill people. There was little awareness that the majority of ex-patients had treatable mental illnesses. Mental health charities fought long and hard to remedy the situation but with a continued lack of funding it was an uphill battle.

Therapeutic Communities

Therapeutic communities are places where therapists and patients live together in a community setting. The first were set up in the 1940's. The community is self-functioning and self-governing. Patients learn to cope with addictions, behavioural or emotional problems.

HMP Grendon Underwood in Buckinghamshire is such a community but in a prison setting. It was opened in 1962 "*as an experimental psychiatric prison to provide treatment for prisoners with antisocial personality disorders*". Five therapeutic communities operate separately within the prison.

Two Butler national prison awards have been won for work being carried out with prisoners at Grendon. Prisoners who choose to serve their sentence at Grendon must agree to stay for at least 2 years. They must be committed to being drug free and have a genuine desire for personal change.

This kind of therapeutic community is not, as might be thought, an easy alternative to standard prisons. Days are highly structured consisting of therapeutic classes interspersed with chores such as gardening and cleaning. It reflects normal community life as far as is possible.

Art therapies are particularly encouraged. Group therapy, women's and men's groups and group psychotherapy are available to teach patients the social skills required for successful integration into their community when they leave prison. Better have someone re-integrate than become bitter, isolated and therefore prone to re-offending.

Rehabilitation Units

Rehabilitation Units are a cross between psychiatric hospitals and therapeutic communities. Residents have to commit to living in the unit for the duration of their therapy; from 18 months to 2 years. The new unit I visited was well designed in a homely way with comfortable sitting rooms, domestic furniture and kitchens with domestic (rather than industrial) equipment. Each resident was allocated a private room with cabling for TV and the internet.

New residents would have medication monitored until the symptoms of their illness levelled out and they were able to start their therapeutic work in the unit.

The Unit Manager had practical plans for encouraging residents to take part in regular activities such as college classes, social clubs, voluntary or paid part time work. These activities would teach residents a mix of social and psychological skills necessary for successful independent living.

Examples for basic social skills might be:

- prompting to take medication
- get up and dressed [personal hygiene & time management]
- encouragement to get on transport for class, social club or work [confidence building]
- completing application forms for appeals or employment

The intended staff for this Unit ranged from psychiatric nurses to health care staff and generalist mental health workers. Each patient would be assigned a specific key worker. I was informed that local residents were very supportive of the scheme, which makes it more likely to succeed.

The manager was enthusiastic about seeing patients emerging as unique characters out of the psychotic and emotional clouds which hid their true nature. Sadly, for reasons I cannot repeat here, his lacklustre NHS employers lost a fine caring manager.

Case Studies

IMPORTANT - please read the following notes before commencing this chapter.

The next chapter comprises the case histories but to make you work a bit harder I am including exercises in diagnosis which you might like to try. BUT please remember before doing this:

- these exercises are for fun to give you a taste of medical diagnosis. **THEY ARE NOT TO QUALIFY YOU TO DIAGNOSE PROFESSIONALLY NOR TO OFFER A DIAGNOSIS TO AN ILL PERSON.**

- I have included in this edition other theoretical standpoints so that you will be aware that 'diagnosis' in the traditional sense only applies to clinicians.

- **NONE OF MY CASE STUDIES REPRESENT REAL PEOPLE.** They are vignettes (combinations) of patients and people I have met during my life which demonstrate the individual elements of diagnosis.

- Confidentiality is the hallmark of all mental health workers. That means NEVER revealing information you have learned during the course of your work. There are strict laws governing personal privacy not least the principles of working in an ethical way which underpin this kind of work.

- Please do not practice the following exercises on anyone, not even friends or family. They are for demonstration purposes only and not meant to constitute professional training.

"[diagnoses] can consign individuals to ..scorn ..
& . ..physical & emotional abuse"
Martha Minow

Chapter 11

Case Studies

This chapter includes:
[Readers attention is drawn to footnotes in the previous chapter]
Why I started My Personal Journey of Understanding
How I Arrived At My Personal View
How Symptoms of Mental Illness Resemble Everyday Experience
Exercise in Diagnosis Using A Case History
CASE HISTORIES (each contains: symptoms, types, causes, cures/remedies)
Brief Psychotic Disorder
Depressive Illness
Eating Disorders
Mania
Obsessive Compulsive Disorder (OCD)
Personality Disorders
• Autism & Solitude
• 8 types of personality disorder
Phobias
Schizophrenia
• Positive & negative faces of Schizophrenia
• Social Withdrawal & Sensory Input
• Cultural Factors and Diagnosis

Please read the footnotes at the end of the previous chapter before starting this chapter.

In this chapter I would like to look at illustrations of a range of mental illnesses. Not everyone in the field shares the view that we should diagnose because diagnosis is really a medical model. I have organised this chapter so that you can have a flavour of several views but remember these vignettes (character portraits) are listed around basic diagnoses, for example depressive illness.

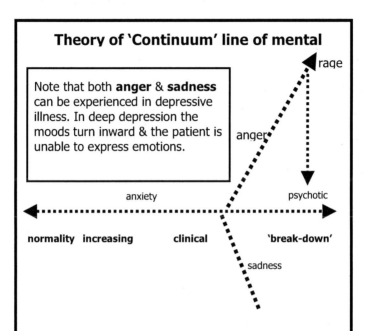

Theory of 'Continuum' line of mental

Note that both **anger** & **sadness** can be experienced in depressive illness. In deep depression the moods turn inward & the patient is unable to express emotions.

rage

anger

anxiety

psychotic

normality increasing   **clinical**   **'break-down'**

sadness

We **all** move along a line[continuum] between extreme poles of mood / behaviour. That is not to say that we will reach an extreme [clinical depression or psychosis] but the <u>potential</u> is there.

Why some people reach extremes depends on many factors:

» **life events** [what happens to us - tragedy, trauma]
» **genetics** [inherited tendency to mental ill health]
» **environment** [our experiences of people & places]
» **adaptation** [difficulty in adapting to circumstances]

Some patients develop physical not mental symptoms when stressed e.g. heart attack, stroke, viral infection, back pain. These are outward signs of the same stress factors.

In other words, mental illness is NOT a sign of weakness [urban myth] but a way the body can become ill.

Just a reminder, none of these represent real people, living or dead; they are amalgams of situations and characteristics that I have brought together to illuminate the diagnoses for you. Most people do not experience their symptoms permanently but in episodes which may happen weeks, months or even years apart. This is why I frown on terms such as 'depressive' or 'schizophrenic', which deny the existence of the person behind the diagnosis and the life they lead between episodes of illness.

My Personal Journey of Understanding

I have always been an analytical person and so this type of thinking was second nature to me. I believe that people who have had a dysfunctional childhood will naturally become analytical, and that will become a lifelong trait. Children are curious about what is happening to them and want to know why, especially when that something is not a good experience. If I could understand what was happening inside my brain:

- I would lose my fear of mental illness (and the symptoms can be very frightening)
- I would be able to control the symptoms more
- I would begin to notice earlier if I was becoming unwell

How I Arrived At My Personal View

Even before starting work in the field of adult mental health I had many ideas about the symptoms I had experienced during my episodes of mental illness. These ideas were confirmed by the excellent supervisor I was given years later, who also believed mental illness was on a continuum, in other words all of us at

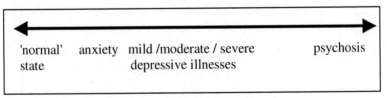

| 'normal' state | anxiety | mild /moderate / severe depressive illnesses | psychosis |

some time might experience symptoms.

This is not to say EVERYONE will become psychotic! But, it means there is not a specific type of human who will develop mental illness and another who will not. Notice that I have drawn the scale on the previous page with a double headed arrow.

This is to demonstrate that even at the far end of the scale there is a way back to normality [whatever being normal means]. It is my belief that the symptoms of any mental illness are no different, except in degree, to everyday human experiences. These are examples of what I mean:

Symptoms of Mental Illness & Everyday Experiences

Symptom	Similar Everyday Experience
OCD - checking & testing	ever closed a front door, had a feeling you had forgotten to lock it or switch off the oven? Doing this 1/2 times is considered 'normal'- in OCD it is continuous.
isolation	enduring isolation of bereavement, or someone you love moving away
mania - euphoria	euphoria in passing an examination, winning something, falling in love; imagine this happens day after day, until you are exhausted
hallucination	normal process of 'seeing' people you love after they have died
voice hearing	hearing something but not being sure you heard it can cause huge anxiety
psychosis - (paranoia)	if you have been bullied, or fearful about a family crisis or undergone surgery which was defective; the anxiety you felt is not as powerful as constant paranoia. Imagine a nightmare that happens all day
	imagine the shock of hearing very bad

depression	news and being unable to take it in - sort of shock and inertia; helpless feelings

Exercise in Diagnosis Using A Case History

The first page of each case history contains the symptoms, causes and cure from DSMIV the clinicians diagnostic manual. I will use the following standard symbols:

■ symptom ♣ cause ➢ cure

I have completed an exercise in diagnosis for you in 'brief psychotic disorder'. Thereafter, you might like to try it for yourself.

Brief Psychotic Disorder

Brief Psychotic Disorder is the medical term for what many people term nervous breakdown. During psychosis a patient's perception recedes under delusions and hallucinations which alter their sense of reality. Life is highly disorganised because patients can neither think logically nor separate the real from the delusional world. Simple tasks such a washing, dressing, working or remembering to take medication are impossible.

Can you remember a children's toy called a kaleidoscope? It consisted of two telescope-like tubes with coloured pieces of transparent acetate or crystals inside. These formed the patterns you could see as the tubes were twisted. Between each pattern formation there is a period of darkness before the next pattern appears. Imagine psychosis as the darkness and sanity as the pattern which forms as the darkness moves aside.

Life is never quite the same after psychosis because any life experience changes you. However, sometimes the patterns can be richer and brighter and the smallest things in life can give you greater pleasure as you come to appreciate the peace of sanity.

Symptoms:

Physical

- speech disorganised
- symptoms of withdrawal - similar to catatonic schizophrenia
- dishevelled appearance

Mental

- hallucinations – seeing or hearings things that no one else can
- inability to concentrate
- extreme fear

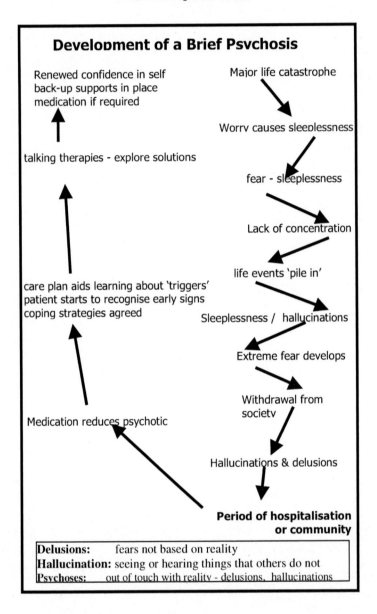

Development of a Brief Psychosis

Renewed confidence in self
back-up supports in place
medication if required

Major life catastrophe

Worry causes sleeplessness

talking therapies - explore solutions

fear - sleeplessness

Lack of concentration

life events 'pile in'

care plan aids learning about 'triggers'
patient starts to recognise early signs
coping strategies agreed

Sleeplessness / hallucinations

Extreme fear develops

Withdrawal from
society

Medication reduces psychotic

Hallucinations & delusions

**Period of hospitalisation
or community**

Delusions: fears not based on reality
Hallucination: seeing or hearing things that others do not
Psychoses: out of touch with reality - delusions, hallucinations

■ delusions – strong fixed ideas or beliefs which do not match reality

Causes

Generally attributed to one or more of the following:

♣ any major life stress or series of stresses
♣ following the trauma of childbirth
♣ a symptom of psychotic depressive illness

Cures or Remedies

➢ medication - anti psychotics
➢ detainment in psychiatric hospital
➢ given time and peace brief psychosis can heal itself

****

Look out for the corresponding bullets in the description of the illness;

■ symptom   ♣ cause   ➢ cure

I have marked these in this first case history.

Case History for Brief Psychotic Disorder - Jane

"If I knew I had to go through this again, I would kill myself. It was like hell. I really believed 'they' were following me trying to control my mind ■. Everyone was in the plot even the doctor and my husband. It was a nightmare only the nightmare was happening during the day." Jane is 40 and separated after years of marriage. Neither the marriage nor Jane's childhood were happy ♣. She had no family, lived a solitary existence with a mundane job that she hated.

Joe, one of her friends, noticed Jane had left her answer phone on and had not replied to his usual calls ■. When he called at her flat after work, the curtains were closed and he noticed an upstairs light on even though it was light outside ■. Joe rang Cynthia, a mutual friend. Cynthia said Jane had not been to evening classes, which was unusual ■ as this was Jane's only regular outing.

Next morning Joe and Cynthia called Jane's employer who said she had been acting differently to normal ■ over the past few weeks, withdrawing. A personnel officer had called to the house several times without seeing any signs of life.

Joe and Cynthia called the police. A warrant was obtained for them to enter Jane's house. A police officer and social worker met Joe and Cynthia at the house. After ringing the bell for some time Jane answered the door. Her friends were shocked by her appearance; wild and dishevelled ■. Jane looked terrified. She refused to allow the police inside but reluctantly admitted the others.

The house was a mess. Cynthia tried to hug Jane but she backed off and crouched in a chair staring at something she could see ■ but no one else in the room could. Jane said she had been to see her doctor but had to rush out as a man in the waiting room was listening to everything she was telling her GP ■ . All this was very real to Jane ■.

The social worker took Joe and Cynthia aside and said Jane would have to be detained under the Mental Health Act and taken to hospital ➤. Joe asked if he could take her as he knew sectioning might affect Jane's career. After an hour of coaxing Jane was persuaded to go. Cynthia was allowed to stay in her dormitory until the medication sent Jane to sleep.

In the morning when the psychiatrist arrived, Jane began to show signs of fear again. Some medication ➤ was prescribed and a mental nurse gave Jane a tablet which she refused. One of the other nurses asked Jane why she was not taking the medication. Jane said the psychiatrist was trying to poison her ■. Jane's belief was so strong that she could not be persuaded until the first nurse returned and injected Jane with a drug which put her to sleep.

Cynthia and Joe visited Jane regularly over the next few weeks, and noticed she was improving. Jane was given counselling ➤ and medication ➤. Several months later, Jane was discharged and continued to see the counsellor ➤. She was embarrassed by what had happened.

Almost a year later, Jane found the confidence to try a more interesting job ➤ and began to build a new life. The symptoms of the psychosis did not return.

****

Therapeutic Inputs for Brief Psychotic Disorder

For this type of mental illness it is vital that medication is given for the symptoms of psychosis, (visual and verbal hallucinations, delusions). Brain chemistry cannot be altered by counselling (although some people claim this to be possible).

Although there is a school of thought that says all psychosis has meaning, someone at this depth of mental distress would be unable to respond to logical explanations and this would only prolong their suffering.

In the days before medication psycho-analysis was used as a curative. Jung himself dealt with his own psychotic symptoms by analysing the phenomena but remember he was an exceptionally gifted person and secondly we only have his anecdotal evidence for what happened during his period of illness.

The definition of psychosis is being out of touch with reality so whatever stimulus is given to the patient will become part of their delusional world. As recovery starts, supportive counselling can help to build confidence. Analytical therapy is not generally recommended at this point, as the patient needs to build confidence analyses which might accentuate their distress.

&&&&&&&&&&&&&&&&&&&&&&&&&&&&&

Depressive Illness

The adjective depressed is often wrongly used to describe sadness e.g. "I was really depressed" meaning 'I was very sad'. The difference between sadness and depression is like the difference between a cold and pneumonia. Depressive illness is common with about 1 in 4 people treated at some time during their life.

Prisoners in solitary confinement, refugees, soldiers in battle, major accident victims, pregnant women and the recently bereaved are likely to become depressed.

Suicidal Urges

Severe depressive illness can be lethal. People of all ages and all backgrounds take their own lives. Suicidal urges are symptoms of severe depression. Sometimes, a patient's lack of energy prevents them attempting suicide. The danger time comes as their energy levels start to rise, so this is the time for vigilance.

Symptoms:

At least 5 of the following must be present almost every day:

Physical

- sleep disturbances (lack of, or increase of)
- lack of energy
- decrease or increase in physical movements
- changes to weight and appetite (increase or decrease)
- withdrawal from activity and social life

Mental

- persistently low mood (irritability in children and teens.)
- tearfulness
- lack of concentration or decisiveness
- lack of pleasure in everyday life and activity
- feelings of guilt or worthlessness

138

- thoughts or desire of death

Causes:

- ♣ devastating life events
- ♣ loss e.g. bereavement, amputation, job, relationship
- ♣ family history of the illness
- ♣ isolation
- ♣ changes in brain chemistry
- ♣ long term and severe abuse of alcohol or drugs

This is a common illness, affecting about 5% of women and 2 – 3% of men.

Cures or Remedies

- ➢ medication which re-balances brain chemistry
- ➢ talking cures - psychotherapy or counselling
- ➢ cognitive-behavioural therapy
- ➢ electro convulsive therapy

Using this system of bullets, see if you can mark symptoms, cause and cure within this case study (follow my example - brief psychotic disorder);

■ symptom   ♣ cause   ➢ cure

Case History for Depressive illness - Sally

"It was like being at the bottom of a deep pit. No ladder was long enough to reach down and help pull me out. All the time, I felt I had a shadow following me – my black shadow. Even when I was sitting comatose in a chair at home I was aware of friends visiting. I couldn't respond but all the time I was saying to myself 'for God's sake don't leave me alone'.

It was the most isolating experience I have suffered in my life. Every day I had the repeated thought that it would be better not to wake up but I was just to tired to do anything about it."

Sally had reached her 56th birthday. Several times she had tried talking to counsellors. Sally never liked to talk about her feelings and would break off therapy. Sally had suffered so long that she had almost become used to her illness which she called her black shadow. She was one of many people who give their depression a name as if it were a tangible object. Winston Churchill called his, his black dog.

Sally's mother had depressive illness and died young after a very unhappy life. Sally often thought about her mother. She regarded her mother's life as being wasted and was angry with both parents for her own unhappy childhood. Sally was married to John a kind man but one who found it difficult to talk about feelings. When she became depressed John would anxiously try to do things for her rather than talk. He found it difficult to understand what was happening.

Over a period of several months Sally had become withdrawn and so low in mood that John was afraid for her. If he tried to talk to her she snapped back or burst into tears. Sally would sit around for long periods doing nothing and the house became dirtier.

Sally no longer had the energy or inclination to make love with John and rejected his advances. John felt rejected and stopped trying after a few months. He started an affair with a colleague and tried to avoid Sally by going out to the pub after work. Sometimes he came home drunk.

Whereas most people would feel alert after sleeping all night, Sally woke from her restless sleep feeling heavy and tired. Most of the night she lay awake thinking; repeated thoughts about the worthlessness of her life. When Sally's friends visited she would sit in her chair not responding. Most of them stopped calling because they couldn't cope with seeing her suffering and so she felt unwanted and isolated.

Eventually Sally stopped bothering to get up. Feeling desperate Sally knew she wanted to die. She had no energy to do anything and her dark thoughts held her deeper in depression.

John took the bull by the horns and insisted Sally went with him to their GP. Sally's GP prescribed anti-depressants and made an appointment for her to see a psychiatrist. John and Sally were reluctant to go to the psychiatric hospital. The GP reassured them this was a special hospital for people with mental health problems and she would only be attending as a day patient.

John asked how long Sally's treatment would take but the GP was not able to give him an exact time; it would depend upon Sally's response. The GP wanted John to be involved in Sally's treatment and she agreed.

Sally attended as an outpatient for several months. She and the psychologist discovered that many of her difficulties went back to her childhood days. Sally's recovery was erratic. Once or twice she slipped back into depression. However she was reassured by staff and agreed on one occasion to be admitted into hospital. At the same time, John found the courage to seek counselling for himself and was relieved when he started to talk about his feelings. It made things easier at home.

As Sally recovered she and John realized that they needed to separate. The marriage was no longer working. Although it was a sad decision they knew it was best for both of them and agreed to remain in contact. She did have further episodes of depression but over a long period of time started coping with them better and asking for help at an earlier stage.

****

Other Therapeutic Inputs for Depressive Illness

Cognitive Behavioural Therapy (CBT)

Mild to moderate depression is often treated with cognitive behavioural therapy. This teaches the patient the links between thinking, feeling and behaviour. Although initial thoughts might arise over which they have no control, what they can change is the subsequent thoughts. If they challenge the initial though, then feelings and behaviour (what they do) will change. Let me give you an example, using Sally's case.

Sally would be encouraged to keep a written record of her thoughts, feelings and subsequent behaviours. This is not easy to do at first, which is why it needs an experienced practitioner who knows how to overcome any problems which arise, including the difficulty of remembering the thoughts. Notice that the initial or naturally arising thought is the same in both cases. We cannot control the initial thought which arises from the unconscious (out of awareness) part of mind.

Before Therapy

Initial Thought:	it's grey. My life will always be sad
subsequent feeling:	feels sad and hopeless
behaviour:	stays in bed and feels worse

After Cognitive Behavioural Therapy (CBT)

Initial Thought:	it's grey. My life will always be sad
thought challenge:	why should it be? I have good days. It isn't bad every day.
subsequent feeling:	feels a slight relief
behaviour:	gets up even if tired and makes tea.
subsequent feeling:	feels better so goes out for a walk

Green Therapies

Self help or green therapies would be administered at the mild to moderate stages of depression. Sally would be encouraged to read about depression so that she fully understands what is happening to her. In Primary Care, the model of care for depression is partly chemical (treated with medication) and partly environmental (looking at life events). Sally might be offered a green book prescription, books which help her understand depressive illness and how medication will help. There is plenty of material on the internet and if Sally was computer literate she might be encouraged to find materials herself and discuss these with a mental health worker.

Green Gym

Green gyms are relatively new but increasing in popularity. I covered how they operate in an earlier chapter. Exercise is recommended for depressive illness as it increases hormones called endorphins, which help to increase mood enhancing chemicals in the brain. Depression is very isolating and knowing people understand can be very beneficial (although someone in deep depression may not want to be around other people).

Therapeutic Community

Practitioners in therapeutic communities treat depressive illness by encouraging participation in community activity or art therapies. People with depression are known to get better when they feel needed and have meaningful occupation. A therapeutic community or therapeutic activity can offer these.

Psycho Analysis or Analytical Counselling Models

Psychoanalysts or analytical models offer the patient the opportunity to explore their early life in order to understand where their present day problems originate. The theory is that when a patient understands why they behave as they do, they can begin to change their maladaptive behaviour and their symptoms will disappear.

However, analysis can be emotionally painful as patients come to terms with their early life and this has to be taken into consideration when selecting this type of therapy. Patients usually feel worse before they improve with analyses.

Solution Focused Therapies (SFT)

Solution focused therapies are supportive, create a positive environment and build self esteem. I know it to be very effective in mild to moderate and even severe depression. However, I would always persuade the patient to see their GP for medication if the depression was severe.

The skill is a <u>very</u> delicate approach in trying to get depressed patients to remember successes. If they cannot, it is vital the therapist finds a way of ensuring the patient does not feel they have 'failed' which can add to their sense of failure. This is the skill in what might seem a simple type of therapy.

I would prime the patient, explaining the intervention needs persistence. SFT is based on a therapeutic alliance between therapist and patient; encouraging patient success (hope). The emphasis is on success rather than dwelling on past failures.

We would monitor mood by a simple self scoring 0 - 10 (0 worst mood and 10 best mood). I might encourage the patient to write a mood diary or personal journal as a resource.

&&&&&&&&&&&&&&&&&&&&&&&&&&&&&

Eating Disorders

Anorexia means restricting intake of food whereas bulimia is binge-eating and purging (by laxatives or self-induced vomiting). There are some aspects of both behaviours in many eating disorders so doctors do not now tend to separate the diagnoses. It is not that these patients do not want to eat because they are often obsessed by food and crave it. However, the drive not to eat or to purge are impossible to control and often frighten the patient.

Do you remember thinking you were fat as a teenager and when you were older you looked at your photos and thought you looked normal? It's a sort of mental trick being played in the minds of people with eating disorders. It is extremely difficult for families to understand when teenagers weighing less than 6 stones see themselves as fat.

This illness is misunderstood even among medical staff. Eating-disordered patients do not always receive the sympathetic approach they need. Brute force feeding does not work because patients are cunning in getting rid of the food they are given in hospital. Nagging does not help either. Many patients fear their own lack of control around food and want to be cured but are unable to do this by themselves.

Imagine seeing your daughter or son starving themselves to death and you can do nothing. Even clinicians find it hard to treat these patients, knowing that 25% of the young people (generally) who are admitted to hospital for treatment will eventually die of multiple organ failure.

Symptoms:

Occurrence is about 1 –3% of the population. Generally 2 episodes a week for 3 months of these symptoms:

Physical
- body weight fluctuation
- self induced recurrent vomiting or purging
- or restricting intake of food
- tooth decay (because of stomach acids from vomiting)
- menstrual cycles disrupted and may disappear

Mental
- fear of gaining weight (anorexia)
- body shape becomes obsessive
- belief that they are being judged by physical appearance

Causes
- ♣ obsession with thinness especially in fashion

♣ history of family problems

♣ fear of growing up and facing independence

♣ bullying or teasing at school especially about appearance

♣ desire to control themselves or their families

♣ devastating experience such as rape

♣ family physical or psychological abuse

♣ self loathing

Cures or Remedies

➢ compulsory hospitalization with strict feeding regime

➢ psychotherapy

➢ group therapy

➢ media and psychiatrists liaising with media about mis-representation in books and magazine of body image

****

Using this system of bullets, see if you can mark symptoms, cause and cure within this case history (follow my example - brief psychotic disorder);

■ symptom   ♣ cause   ➢ cure

Case History for Eating Disorders - Marilyn

Marilyn slouched into the office. Just behind the thin skin in her face I could see the outline of her skull and blueness around her hollowed eyes, her teeth mottled from the years of vomiting. It was nothing like the photograph her mum showed me of Marilyn at 12 years of age.

This was a young woman of 24. She had been unemployed for some years after contracting her eating disorder and lived at home with her parents. She had always wanted a family but the boy she loved had left her for someone else and this had shattered her world. Her menstrual cycle had ceased and her GP was getting worried about organ damage so he insisted she went into hospital.

On the ward Marilyn was weighed every day, along with all the other girls. When meals arrived one of the nurses would sit with them to prevent food being hidden, as it always was. Her friend Fay had recently been discharged and Marilyn wanted to go home as well but the doctors refused as she was at a very dangerously low weight. Marilyn had been eating all the food but then vomiting it into various places in and outside the ward. She consistently refused to attend for psychotherapy.

Later that week, she went with Fay to see the body of their friend Cassie. Both of them were shocked when they saw the tiny wasted figure being made ready for the undertakers. Fay started going to therapy after that, but Marilyn refused.

She was in hospital for several months before they allowed her to go home. Despite all her mother's care, Marilyn was unable to keep up her eating schedule and died later that spring.

****

Someone like Marilyn could not be forced to attend therapy unless her life was in danger, although doctors might insist she was hospitalised to stabilise her weight. No one can motivate a patient, so force is counter productive. Unless there is motivation, the patient ceases therapy within a very short time. It is much like dieting in that respect.

Cognitive Behavioural Therapy

CBT therapists would look at Marilyn's attitude towards eating. The therapist would encourage Marilyn to keep a food diary and to start eating small amounts of extra foods each week. No food would be 'forbidden' (as tends to happen on diets) as forbidden foods rapidly become objects of obsession. As NLP therapists say, 'whatever you resist, persists'.

The diaries would log the time and amount of food, whether it was a binge/ purge, together with details of what the patient was

147

thinking and feeling at the time. 'Catching' thoughts and feelings is not meant to be punitive but a way of the patient and therapist together examining what happened in order to try to plan a new strategy. The therapist would be looking for alternative thoughts, acceptable to the patient, which might:

- help the patient see if they were using food to replace feelings
- the circumstances under which this was happening
- what might be done differently e.g. instead of eating, breaking a glass when feeling angry

Over time, several weeks or months, the patient would be helped to find a more productive relationship with the food, and other ways of dealing with their pain, frustrations, emotions and problems.

Solution Focused Therapy

A solution focused therapist would help Marilyn to focus on what she wanted out of life. It would be her choice whether or not she wanted to concentrate on the part food played in her life. However, even if it did not start out this way, I am sure a food issue would surface in other ways.

If Marilyn did choose to look at her dysfunctional eating habits, then the SFT therapist might use similar tactics to the CBT methodology - food diaries, encouragement, planning goals and reviewing outcomes (results) regularly. Scaling is used very often in SFT, usually simple 0 to 10 scale which is infinitely adaptable.

If Marilyn chose to look at other areas in her life then a successful outcome whatever the area would most probably result in a beneficial change in her eating habits.

I saw a cartoon which illustrated bingeing beautifully. It was a naked man, gazing anxiously into a full fridge in the middle of the night. It was entitled 'feelings in the fridge'.

Analytical Therapies

Analytical therapists would concentrate on Marilyn's life experience, particularly in childhood. The analyst would help Marilyn to recognise where her current life difficulties lay.

Again, not necessarily directly to do with food and eating; these are often symbolic ways of dealing with life's problems - for example, filling with food, alcohol or drugs are common ways of avoiding dealing with emotions. The physical body is so busy digesting there is no room for unbearable feelings. Unfortunately the pay-off is pretty disastrous for the person's own psyche (spiritual well-being).

&&&&&&&&&&&&&&&&&&&&&&&&&&&&&

Mania

Many creative people develop this illness which is characterized by periods of intense activity, irrational thinking and erratic moods. Dr Kay Redfield (an American psychiatrist) describes the disorder in her book 'Touched with Fire'. There is an excellent biography called 'Daughter of the Queen of Sheba' in which Jackie Lyden describes a chaotic and traumatic life with her mother who had recurring episodes of mania.

The illness can exist as a separate entity but this is less common. When coupled with depression it is called bi-polar or manic-depression. 'Bi-polar' refers to the extremes of the mood; mania and depression.

Mania cannot be controlled and is frightening to the patient. The brain chemistry is firing off at speed and only medication can bring the patient down off their high. Do you remember the fairy tale of the girl with the magic dancing shoes who finally danced herself to death? The body needs rest in a manic state but the brain says no.

There is another form in which the patient, out of their usual character, becomes extremely irritable and arrogant. Thoughts are affected and patients can develop grandiose plans to do things which are impossible on a practical level.

Patient's can spend uncontrollably whilst high. Others may have unquenchable sexual appetites which they indulge only to recoil in horror at what they have done when they return to sanity.

Families can be destroyed; patients filled with embarrassment and anguish. Families are often worn out with dealing with their loved-one's illness, particularly as there is usually no warning of when an episode will occur.

Symptoms:

Physical

- increase in energy - psychomotor agitation
- marked increase in activity levels
- decreased need for sleep

Mental

- patient has a highly inflated opinion of him/her self (grandiosity)
- very talkative
- lack of concentration
- may indulge in sprees of sexual activity, buying or investing
- fear of an 'out of control' situation but unable to control it
- rapid swings of mood

Causes:

- ♣ imbalance of brain chemistry
- ♣ family history of the illness (genetic factors)
- ♣ over reaction to recovering from a period of depression
- ♣ abuse of alcohol or drugs

Cures or Remedies

> ➤ Medications which change the brain chemistry
> ➤ Talking therapies, cognitive behavioural or solution focused.

****

Using this system of bullets, see if you can mark symptoms, cause and cure within this case history (follow my example - brief psychotic disorder);

■ symptom   ♣ cause   ➤ cure

Case History for Mania - Esmerelda

"I'm coming down now over the last day or so. I try to enjoy the mood when comes on. There's usually no warning just a buzzy feeling like champagne bubbles in my blood. Things start to get better. Even the grass is brighter and greener. I have tremendous bursts of energy and you know I feel I can do anything!"

"I went shopping last time." She points to her wardrobe which is bursting at the seams with garish clothing, clearly unsuitable for someone of 55. "Look at that lot! The credit-card company was furious! It 3 years now and I'm still paying. I'll never clear it now. What's the point."

"And I keep picking up these men. You know, one night stands. It's really great at first, the sex, then I get uncomfortable but it goes on and on. They are scared of me then and I get mad and shout. I want to sleep but I keep pacing up and down the room. And now I think I have VD."

She breaks off, laughs mirthlessly and fetches a glass of water and a bottle of pills. "There. You see, it's hard to remember. Lithium. Balances me but look at this." She holds out her hand; it is shaking visibly. "Been like that for years. I won't take them again, I just can't. I feel dead inside."

"I've lived two lives and not enjoyed one of them. I know they make fun of me out there, think I'm an old drama queen. If they only knew what it was really like. I'm scared inside, exhausted."

She bursts into uncontrollable sobs. I can't think of anything to say to comfort her. I try to understand what her relatives must be suffering. Her mother is 81, exhausted, her sister has disowned her.

Esmerelda lives with her mother in social housing, having lost the family home to the bank. Her mother does not know what to do and is clearly at the end of her tether. Marilyn is due in court for dangerous driving and she knows she will lose her license this time because of her illness. They will be really isolated then and I fear that Marilyn or her mother might take their life.

****

Some treatments like lithium are not pleasant and after some years can lead to shaking of the hands (Parkinsonism) or kidney problems. It is difficult to retain a medication regime not only because of the side effects but also the psychological impact of knowing you must take a drug or cocktail of drugs every day for the rest of your life. Patients often enjoy the high at first, and many do not recognise that they are ill.

Cognitive Behavioural Therapy

A CBT therapist might effectively deal, in Esmerelda's case, with her refusal to take her prescribed medication and consequent cycles of becoming ill. They would look at her reasons for refusing and the consequences for both Esme and her mother.

Remember, CBT is about linking thoughts to feelings and behaviour. If a patient considers (thinking) what will happen if they don't take medication that might change their attitude (feelings) and therefore resulting (behaviour) will be different.

&&&&&&&&&&&&&&&&&&&&&&&&&&&&

Obsessive Compulsive Disorder (OCD)

We all have times when we check doors are locked before going out. Perhaps if we are stressed we might even go back and check again. But if checking can become obsessional. Obsessive compulsive disorder is difficult to understand. It is a very unusual disorder but there are three common elements:

Obsession – with anything; in my case study, fear of contamination

Compulsion – this develops from the obsession. In my case study, hand washing seems the solution to the obsession but this soon leads to compulsive body washing. This is not normal hygiene; washing goes on several hours leaving the skin broken and bleeding

Ritual – as the compulsion develops, it begins to become ritualistic. For example, the patient will not go out until they have washed a certain number of times. If the ritual is performed incorrectly the patient obsessively starts the whole process again, sometimes to the stage of exhaustion. Rituals can last for hours and take over everyday life.

Symptoms:

It is not a common illness occurring in 1.5 to 2% of the population in a year.

Mental – Obsessions

- 1: persistent idea – e.g. the house is contaminated
- 2: persistent thought – e.g. burglars are going to raid their home
- 3: persistent image – e.g. thinking of crude sexual acts

Physical – Compulsions

Compulsions are repetitive actions outside the patient's control. The actions become ritualised, i.e. have to be done a certain number of times, in a certain order. The patient cannot control the rituals which start taking over their life.

The examples below refer to the respective numbered examples above:

- compulsive ritual for 1: e.g. constant hand washing
- compulsive ritual for 2: e.g. repeated checking and testing of locks and doors
- compulsive ritual for 3: e.g. praying to negate guilt

Causes:

- ♣ imbalance in brain chemistry
- ♣ life trauma

Cures or Remedies

- ➢ Cognitive-Behavioural therapy
- ➢ medication can also help

Patients are given a therapeutic programme which gradually reduces the amount of time spent on the ritual.

****

Using this system of bullets, see if you can mark symptoms, cause and cure within this case history (follow my example - brief psychotic disorder);

■ symptom   ♣ cause   ➢ cure

Case History for Obsessive Compulsive Disorder (OCD) - Cynthia

Walking into Cynthia's home was like walking into shop. Piles of

154

boxes on the floor, jobs half completed. Cynthia's immaculate hair seemed lacquered into place but her makeup was roughly put on. As we spoke I noticed her glancing regularly into a mirror on the opposite wall brushing back imaginary strands of hair.

"I first started this" she gestured helplessly "type of cleaning about a year ago. At first I wasn't aware of what I was doing. Marjorie, my help, asked if I wanted to dispense with her services. I asked why and she said my standards were too high. I told her she was being silly that the house was grubby and I really needed to give her extra hours."

Cynthia paused then managed a smile. "Well, she was an honest woman. After a week or so of this she sat me down on the sofa and asked me to look around. I had spent all day on my hands and knees rubbing out every spot of dirt from the carpet then at least an hour scrubbing my hands. My hands were raw and bleeding."

Cynthia sat for a while looking at her hands then sighed. "Of course it started soon after Geoff [her husband] died. He died of a chest infection you know. It was five years ago."

She paused again and I nodded. She gestured with her hands obviously unable to speak. "Did you want to scrub away the infection, as if that might bring him back again?" I asked.

"Possibly. I blamed myself really. He had a weak chest but loved his sport. Perhaps the cleaning filled my days so I didn't have to think. Perhaps the dust....I don't know." She sat quietly.

"And now?" I said.

"Now" she replied "I can't control it. I know what I'm doing but I can't help myself."

At that point a red-faced woman opened the front door. It was Marjorie. Cynthia had agreed she could help with the therapy, trying to control the cleaning.

"We will be doing something very different to your usual work schedule Marjorie. It will involve not cleaning and encouraging dirt". Marjorie laughed and Cynthia smiled.

****

Therapy does not always proceed according to plan and often patients will change direction mid way through. The therapist then has to consider whether to adapt the therapy, or if the patient is again trying to avoid the real problem. It is not as simple as it might appear.

Bereavement Counselling

Cynthia has been bereaved for many years but has not come to terms with her husband's death as yet. Some people continue in this state for many years which is a tragedy because they have effectively suspended their lives. However, no one can be forced to deal with loss at what is the wrong time for them.

Two different therapists had tried to get a woman to visit the grave of her mother despite her objections. This was with the best of intentions. It became clear to me that the woman had not yet accepted her mother was dead, so how could she visit the grave?

After working on this, several weeks later she told me of a dream in which her mother had talked to her at length then walked down the garden path closed the gate and waved goodbye. The woman was tearful but said she knew her mother was dead.

I asked if she would like to say something to her mother as a final goodbye. A few days later she was finally able to visit the graveside. Dreams can be useful indicators of what is happening in the patient's unconscious. Jung called dreams 'the royal road to the unconscious'.

Psychotherapy

When a patient enters psychotherapy, they sometimes find it

difficult to know what to say. In this kind of therapy the patient has autonomy to choose what they bring to therapy. Some people find it hard to know where to start because they think all their problems are jumbled up together.

I sometimes explain to patients that we cannot move a mountain; however, if we consider the mountain to be made up of individual pieces of rock, then over time we can move the pieces.

Cynthia may choose to talk about cleaning problems, her obsessions. Equally, she may choose to talk about her husband's death or her own reactions to loss. The initial problem in psychotherapy is not always what the patient decides to deal with.

OCD can be a symptom of something the patient is afraid of facing. Once that has been faced, the obsession might disappear.

Cognitive Behavioural Therapy

If Cynthia attended and asked for help to deal with her OCD, the CBT therapist might proceed in a similar manner as for my eating disorder study. She might be asked to keep a diary of the cleaning, with times and dates and what she was thinking.

From this diary patient and therapist would look for patterns of thinking. For example Cynthia thinking about Bill's death then immediately seeing dust on the carpet it could be either a distraction from an uncomfortable thought or a symbolic reminder. In either way it would not matter because the effect is triggering the problematic cleaning ritual.

Cynthia would be encouraged to examine the thoughts that arose before a cleaning ritual then challenge this thought or find a more positive way of dealing with it. Perhaps she might choose to talk about Bill; small pleasant memories of things they had shared. Eventually, out of this therapy, Cynthia might seek bereavement counselling. A therapist can recommend another type of therapy if it is appropriate and will help the patient.

Behavioural Therapy - Systematic De-sensitisation

There was recently a BBC programme called 'House of Obsessive Compulsives' where people with long-standing OCD lived with a group of therapists over several weeks. During this time each patient was encouraged to face their fear by carrying out a programme of de-sensitisation.

Cynthia might be encouraged to clean for 1 hour and then go out shopping without completing a cleaning cycle. This would raise considerable anxiety at first but would need persistence on behalf of both patient and therapist. This programme would continue until Cynthia felt comfortable and then the time space between cleaning sessions would be reduced again. The process might take several weeks.

The heirarchy of action would be mutually agreed between therapist and patient possibly with the help of a family member or friend. A regular diary would be kept recording the amount of cleaning done and perhaps a score denoting difficulty in doing the task. Over time, cleaning would be reduced.

Note that this behavioural way of conducting therapy does not involve talking about the problem in depth nor trying to discover the cause. In practice, behavioural therapy would rarely be carried out as sole therapeutic input but might be combined, as in cognitive-behavioural therapy.

&&&&&&&&&&&&&&&&&&&&&&&&&&&&

Personality Disorders

There are many kinds of personality disorders. These are very difficult to diagnose or to treat, because generally the patient will be unaware of their behavioural characteristics. All of us have negative characteristics and what passes for normal varies in individuals so who is to say what is acceptable or not in society (providing no danger exists).

In many cases there is a childhood history of abuse perhaps going back many generations. Such children do not know what normal social behaviour is, because it has never been modelled to them. It is not their fault they are the way they are. There is increasing evidence that faulty genes are connected with personality disorders but this science is too new to offer solutions. These patients repeat negative behaviour patterns; wife or husband beating, neurotic behaviours, extreme social isolation leading to hatred of others. However, all murders are not committed either by people with personality disorders or those with a mental illness. Even therapists have sinking hearts when dealing with this group. They are not likeable, pretty people. Sometimes there is nothing to be done in extreme cases where public safety is involved except to lock such people away from the public.

Autism

Autism is a problem that has been uncomfortably included under the banner of personality disorder. Autistic people can be highly intellectually developed or very artistic as well as withdrawing or socially shy. Many clinicians do not like to label people in this way but sometimes labels allow others to develop understanding about the reason for what might seem odd behaviours. For example, autistic children tend to avoid others and find it hard to build close loving relationships. This can lead to feelings of rejection within their own family.

Aspergers is a kind of autism. Aspergers syndrome has only recently been added to the list of diagnoses. Both autistic and Aspergers children are sometimes characterised not only by withdrawal from society but also high intellect and creativity. Have a look at some of the incredible architectural drawings of Stephen Wiltshire, read about savants (prodigies) such as the real 'Rain Man' Kim Peek, or languages expert Daniel Tammett and you will discover some fascinating things about the capabilities of the human mind:

- http://www.stephenwiltshire.co.uk/index.php)
- http://www.guardian.co.uk/science/story/0,3605,1664652,00.
  html
- http://www.guardian.co.uk/weekend/story/0,,1409903,00.htm
  l#article_continue

Solitude

I want to include something positive about solitary lifestyles.
People may dislike social situations or feel uncomfortable around
people for many reasons; perhaps -

- they do not know how to behave in company
- people bully them
- they prefer their own company
- they cannot cope with too many sensory distractions at on
  time e.g. noise, light, colour

It can seem as if such people are from a different planet by those
who do not understand why anyone should shun human company
for lengthy periods of time. However, consider the solitary
lifestyle of artists, writers, composers, philosophers, academics,
or those of monks and nuns. This is a quotation worth
considering. It is from Anthony Storr's book 'Solitude'.

*'Perhaps the ability to distance oneself from over-involvement
with others, and the capacity to make a coherent pattern of one's
life, are important in attaining peace of mind and mental health.'*

Symptoms:

These disorders are generally divided into classes each with its
characteristics. Generally, the individual:

- behaves or reacts in a way markedly different from others
- experiences problems over a wide range of behaviours
- has a long standing condition

Examples of Personality Disorders

- anti social - shuns people and society
- avoidant - inhibited
- borderline– impulsive; finds it hard to form relationships
- dependent - submissive and clinging
- narcissistic - self obsessed
- paranoid - distrustful
- psychopathic - destructive form; unaware of their illness
- schizoid - withdrawing and detached

Physical

No marked physical symptoms.

Causes:

♣ genetic factors
♣ dysfunctional home life from early age

Cures or Remedies

➢ medications to control the symptoms
➢ compulsory hospitalization -sectioning
➢ electro convulsive therapy
➢ psychotherapy
➢ dialectic behavioural therapy

****

Using this system of bullets, see if you can mark symptoms, cause and cure within this case history (follow my example - brief psychotic disorder);

■ symptom   ♣ cause   ➢ cure

Case History for Borderline Personality Disorder -

Tom

Tom has recently been released from prison, his 11th term. He lives on benefits. In the past he has had brief jobs as a dustman, gravedigger, drayman, warehouse operative, railwayman, labourer.

"Never been married, na. I've been alone since I was a nipper. If you told me I'd be in this grim hole all these years I'd have topped myself long since. Thought about that a lot. Well, I've had years of thinking haven't I? Lots of time to stew."

He drags deep on a roll-up and blows the smoke at the ceiling which is cracked with a suggestion of brown ooze. An iron bedstead covered in grubby bedding sags in a corner. A cheap utility wardrobe, dressing table and two wooden chairs (the ones we are sitting on) are the only other furniture.

"I don't know why you're here. Yes, it's all right as long as you don't stop too long. Can't stand company for long. I expect they told you." He drags again and coughs. "What was it like? You mean working? Ah."

"Couldn't settle. Just one job after another. Always some cocky bastard got to me. You know the characters. I dunno". He seems puzzled, rubs his stubbly chin and stares at the floor. "Week here, month there; whole year once. I can't seem to get on. Parents? Ah. Father was ex army, Corporal. Corporal Punishment I called him when I was a lad!"

We share the joke as he laughs and coughs at the same time.

"Yes. A believer in the strap. A strong backhand to the face. Friends? Na. No one allowed at the house. Mother? Little timid woman, mousey sort. Didn't think much of her."

"Love?" He laughs bitterly. For a second I think he's going to cry but he controls it, spits on the floor and drags on the wet end of the roll-up. "Oh, that stuff. He used to land her one regular. Stop him? What for? That's what being married is about, ain't it? When I was older used to land her one myself. That's how it is."

"You mean when I was a kid? I was never one for games, never joined in. Wanted to but it's hard. I used to watch the other kids – sort of sidling up then getting in the game. Cruel little bastards kids. They'd run off if I crept up to them." He laughs harshly.

"Well I learned to bash them instead. Proud? I'll say. It was the only thing I had, my fists. Dad would have been proud of me for that." A tinge of regret crept into his voice. "He's dead so he never knew. The things I done. Going? Now? Well see yer then." He coughs, follows me to the door.

As I walk down the drive I have a sense of him watching me from the other side of the grubby nets. I know he will never admit it but he dreads the years ahead. He knows something is wrong but it's too ingrained to change.

He didn't let me in the following week. I heard later that he was found one morning by the milkman, hanged.

****

&&&&&&&&&&&&&&&&&&&&&&&&&&&

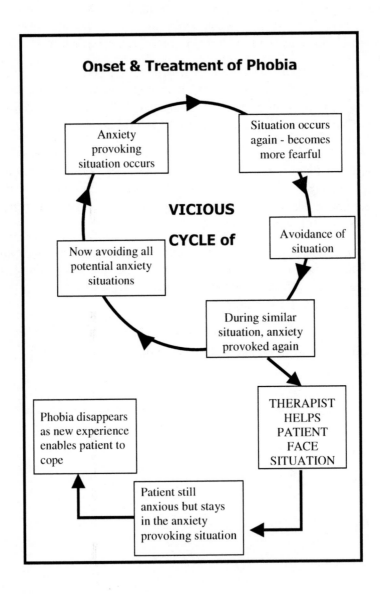

Phobias

Phobia's are excessive fears about objects, things or situations. These fears are strong enough to take over everyday life. Phobias might start specifically e.g. being afraid of the dark, then spreads out into all sorts of fears. Fear is at the root of phobias and often fears that have no specific connection with the type of phobia.

Symptoms:

To be classed as a phobia, the condition must have lasted at least six months.

Physical

There are only the usual physical symptoms connected with anxiety (production of adrenaline).

Mental

- excessive unreasonable fear of an object, thing, or place
- avoidance of facing the fear
- daily living is affected to a marked degree
- the fear is of long standing

Common types of Phobias

- agora – fear of open spaces
- arachna – fear of spiders
- blood/infection – fear of being contaminated
- claustro – fear of being in a confined space
- situational – fear of a specific situation
    e.g. fear of flying, being in lifts
- social – fear of social situations

Causes

- ♣ excessive reaction to negative incidents from the past
- ♣ worsening of an existing fear
- ♣ reaction to a particular loss – e.g. loss of a loved one

♣ reaction to an incident in the distant past

This condition is fairly common, occurring among about 10 – 11% of the population. We all have fears about certain things, but these fears are not considered to be phobias until:

a   that object or thing is regularly avoided
b   the avoidance affects day to day living

Causes are sometimes easy to discover, sometimes more deep-rooted.

Cures or Remedies

> ➢ behavioural therapy
> ➢ psychotherapy
> ➢ cognitive-behavioural therapy

****

Using this system of bullets, see if you can mark symptoms, cause and cure within this case history (follow my example - brief psychotic disorder);

■ symptom   ♣ cause   ➢ cure

Case History for Phobia - Mike

"Its been getting worse over the last few weeks. I used to get to the garden gate and I can't go out the back door now. How long? I've been confined in the house for eight months now."

He is neatly dressed, the house is bright and clean. The only thing you might notice is the bed in the living room. It seems he is living in one room.

"If you'd told me a year ago that I would be afraid to walk outside my own front door, then I could never have believed it." He pauses. "Well, it was after Mary's [his wife] funeral. I got out of the car and looked at the trees. I started to feel faint. The trees seemed to be coming in on me. Plenty of friends turned up.

166

After, we walked back to the cars and I was still feeling dizzy. After that it was a succession of things. At first it was just going to town. Mary and I used to have a bite to eat in a café after shopping, so I tried to do that myself. I couldn't. After that, it got worse until I had to shop locally. I'd tell myself it was ridiculous but that made no difference.

Each time I panicked it was worse the next time. I thought if I stayed in the house it would wear off after a time. I found a home help to do the shopping and moved into this room so I didn't have to go out at all."

He looks really embarrassed and with a voice tinged with anxiety says: "Is there any hope that I'll get over this? I can't bear being confined. It's almost as if I'm in a coffin, like Mary."

He bursts into tears and covers his face with his hands.

****

This is a case where the patient has responded badly to bereavement and in the normal order of things his therapist might recommend bereavement counselling. There is no hard and fast rule, but the over-riding consideration would be what the patient wanted.

Psychotherapy

There are many types of psychotherapy: solution focused, analytical, psycho-dynamic (exploring how relationships from the past have affected current relationships).

It is not necessary to deal directly with the phobia, as would happen in a behavioural approach. A phobia might be seen as symbolic of a life problem. In Mike's case, he has already connected his agoraphobia with Mary's death and sees that he had almost confined himself in the coffin of his room. Listening to what the patient has to say often directs the course of therapy which is why it is important for therapists to be skilled in more than one area of therapy.

Our patient might decide to deal with his anxieties through exploration of his feelings toward life. Or perhaps, if he cannot face talking about the past, a solution focused approach might be more beneficial. Exploratory therapies can often be very painful. Mike, in this instance, would be encouraged to talk about his fears, his hopes and wishes with the aim of discovering what might help him re-gain his zest for life.

Behavioural Therapy

Phobias generally respond well to behavioural therapies, such as systematic de-sensitisation. Mike would be asked to help draw up a list of different stages, perhaps walking to the local shop on his own. The heirarchy might look something like this:

☺ walk to gate with therapist
☺ walk to gate alone
☺ walk to end of road with therapist
☺ walk to end of road alone
☺ walk at the end of road alone, being met by therapist around the next corner

And so on, until he was able to do the whole journey alone.

Sometimes patients like Mike might deal with the phobia and then attend later to deal with the bereavement aspect. It is not necessary to follow a therapeutic path all in one go and many patient do choose to come back in stages, over months or years.

Cognitive-Behavioural Therapy

CBT would be based on much the same lines, but the therapist would concentrate on the thoughts and feelings that resulted from the phobia. A vicious cycle of a phobia will consist of the following elements:

• Initial thought

- resulting thinking
- the responding feeling
- the resulting behaviour

There is a diagram of a typical phobia cycle of a in this chapter.

&&&&&&&&&&&&&&&&&&&&&&&&&&&&&

Schizophrenia

Schizophrenia is a misunderstood illness, not easily diagnosed and not accepted as a distinct condition by many clinicians. It is not a split personality. It is easier to describe by referring to its strange cluster of symptoms which are described later. Schizophrenia is no respecter of persons, age, intellect or social status.

Confusion with Psychopathic Personality Disorder

Very few people with schizophrenia are a danger to the public despite media reports. The public are generally unaware of the difference between paranoid schizophrenia and psychopathic personality disorder.

- **A psychopathic person** is born with no sense of conscience (morals). They cannot 'learn' this because that part of their brain does not respond.

- **People with schizophrenia** do make moral distinctions but act because they are under the influence of powerful delusions such as voices.

Delusions and hallucinations are as real to an ill patient as a living being is to you or I. A patient might absolutely believe he is defending himself from a terrifying enemy who is trying to kill him; but onlookers will see the unprovoked attack on an innocent person. The patient might hear voices directing him/her to harm or kill.

Positive Face of Schizophrenia

If you watch the movie 'A Beautiful Mind' you will see how the genius mathematician John Nash experienced the profound delusional symptoms of schizophrenia yet went on to win a Nobel prize for his work.

The psychologist Rufus May gained his qualification despite living with paranoid schizophrenia. These people demonstrate remarkable achievements in overcoming an illness which shatters perception of the everyday world. Each person has to find a way of coming to terms with their illness.

Negative Face of Schizophrenia

For the few who cannot cope and have no family support, life can be very hard. Unable to perform the basic daily offices of life many people used to end up in prison or wandering as tramps.

Sometimes they committed crimes deliberately because prisons offered a reassuringly regimented life which relieved the chaotic symptoms of the illness.

Symptoms:

Physical

- may show general signs of a lack of personal self care

Mental

- delusions; persistent and irrational thoughts or ideas
       e.g. of murderous attack
- hallucinations; seeing or hearing things that are not there
- speech can be meaningless -'word salad'
- thinking is disordered
- no feelings are apparent
- depression can be a feature
- behaviour is disorganised or non-existent

• anhedonia; inability to gain pleasure from normally pleasurable experiences

The symptoms must be of at least 6 months standing. The cluster of symptoms include audio and visual hallucinations, delusions and loss of identity. The hallucinations and voices are not all destructive; they can be religious, mythological or even amusing. Patients with schizophrenia tend to withdraw socially, or perhaps society withdraws from their perceived strange behaviours.

Social Withdrawal & Sensory Input

I believe social withdrawal can be explained in terms of sensory input levels. We can, as human beings only process a certain amount of input from our senses (vision, audio, touch, taste, smell) at one time.

For example most people can only cope with holding one conversation at a time; remember doing this at a party, and trying to filter out the other noise? Voices and visions can crowd out reality; I will try to demonstrate by asking you to do an exercise in imagination.

Sensory Imagination Exercise

Imagine you are in one of those massive Imax cinemas. The screen measures 21 metres wide by 15 metres tall (about 6 double decker buses) and there are as many as 40 speakers. The curved screen and sound system are designed to surround you with sound and action, such that you have a sense of participating in the movie being shown.

Imagine that your friend in the next seat is trying to have a conversation with you as the movie runs. No chance? Well, maybe you can start to appreciate the sensory overload of auditory and visual hallucinations. They fill the area of sensory perception so full that there is little or no room for anything else. No wonder many people with hallucinations avoid the 'normal' world.

It is only because you cannot see or hear what patients are seeing and hearing, that it is so very difficult to understand the enormity of what is going on inside the mind of someone with schizophrenia. What seems bizarre to you might be quite normal to people with schizophrenia.

Cultural Factors and Diagnosis

This illness needs careful diagnosis as many symptoms are common to other mental illnesses. Some cultures are tolerant and encourage some of the factors which in Western culture could be mis-interpreted as hallucinations and delusions:

- voodoo and witchcraft cultures (e.g. in Haiti)
- religious ecstasies, spiritual images or speaking in tongues
- ancestors 'appear' as living people to advise their relatives
- spiritualists communicate with the dead

A psychiatrist has to take these factors into account when attempting diagnosis. Schizophrenia is also a hugely stigmatised illness which can affect patients ability to find work, another reason for reluctance to diagnose or (on the patient's behalf) to be diagnosed.

Types of Schizophrenia

Catatonic Schizophrenia

Now relatively rare, this type of schizophrenia has the effect of stupefying the individual who sits in a semi-permanent comatose state.

I remember one patient would sit in the same chair hardly moving during the day, eating meals but never speaking. A student nurse

172

made considerable efforts to talk to her about the past and the woman started to respond, only to sink back when this nurse left for another job.

Paranoid Schizophrenia

This type of schizophrenia is distinguished by one specific fearful delusion (false belief). People with this form of the illness can be dangerous if their voices are threatening e.g. directing them to kill. However shocking the acts committed as a result one has to remember this is an illness. In fact, very few patients with this form of the illness commit murder.

Causes

Medical people are not sure of what causes schizophrenia although it is generally believed to be a combination of factors:

- family history of the illness
- current work at the University of Edinburgh is focusing on the genes DISC1 & PDE4B
- breakdown due to prolonged and extreme stress
- environmental stress factors
- traumatic childhood/ family events
- drug-induced schizophrenic-like symptoms

This is the most severe mental illness and there is no known cure although the symptoms can be relieved with medication. Modern medication reduces symptoms enabling many people to lead relatively normal lives.

About 1% of the population is affected by one of these disorders, with onset during adolescence or (more rarely) from middle age.

Cures or Remedies

There is currently no cure for schizophrenia, although drugs relieve the symptoms.

- medications to target faulty brain chemistry
- family work
- cognitive behavioural therapy
- pet therapy

****

Using this system of bullets, see if you can mark symptoms, cause and cure within this case history (follow my example - brief psychotic disorder);

■ symptom   ♣ cause   ➢ cure

Case History for Schizophrenia (early onset) - Mandy

Mandy is an intelligent girl of 20 who has had schizophrenia since she was 15. She lives alone in a small flat and receives a weekly visit from her therapist.

After her initial breakdown she had to leave college because she was unable to cope with the intellectual and social demands. Her boyfriend left her when she was diagnosed because he could not cope with the catastrophic nature of her illness.

"Of course I feel sad about not being able to work. The images are intrusive and the voices so loud I can't concentrate. I set out to do business management and that grieves me too. I just want to be ordinary but I know there is no cure. It took years to accept that.

How did I realize something was wrong? I didn't, my parents did. I started shutting myself off from people. It was difficult to concentrate. I kept feeling this fuzziness in my head as if there was cotton-wool inside of my brain. One day I was on a boat on the Thames looking over at the buildings on the other side. A rip appeared in the sky as if it was a painting and someone had ripped a chunk out of it and there were people in the gap. I couldn't make it out. My friend asked what was wrong. When I told her I saw this shock, as if she didn't see it too. That scared me.

After that things started to get worse. My college work was bad. I'd been working really hard for the exams, perhaps too hard. It was impossible to concentrate with all these weird things going on. I knew I was getting insane but hoping it would go away.

One day at college a voice said Tom was going to kill me. I could see his face changing. He looked scared then his face started to melt. Apparently I grabbed an art knife and tried to stab him. That's when they called someone and I was taken to hospital.

It was such a relief to talk. The doc seemed to understand. I asked if I was mad and he said madness was a term ignorant people used to describe something they don't understand. He said it was possible I was getting schizophrenia. He said the right medication would stop the visions and voices and help me feel normal.

I told him I was scared, that I didn't mean to harm that boy. I asked him if I would be put away and he said it wasn't necessary. As long as I took the medication, things would be fine and someone would visit me to make sure things were OK.

I got very lonely. My parents didn't visit. I suppose it's easier for them. They couldn't cope with it all. I think mum's sister had this so I suppose it brings it back to them.

Tom still visits me. He knows about the voices. They haven't come back since I started taking the tablets. He doesn't seem to mind my flat being messy. I can't get it together to clean up often as I get confused. I kind of hope he visits more often."

****

Family Work

Mental health workers work with the families of people with schizophrenia to try to prevent some of the trauma and disruptions to family life. Many families find it hard to cope with their relative's mood changes and tendency to withdraw which can be misinterpreted as rejection. A son or daughter who appears to change character is very distressing for parents who cannot predict what might happen in the future.

Patients often do not recognise they are ill and refuse medication, so they become ill more often than they should. Lack of drug compliance can lead to family breakdown as the patient's symptoms start to manifest. This is distressful for all concerned.

Family workers encourage regular taking of medication and help the patient prepare a care plan. This is a kind of advance directive made when the patient is well, with directions for how they want to be treated when ill. Plans can be comprehensive and include a patient's list of signs of oncoming episodes of illness, what they want or how they do not want to be treated.

Patients are encouraged to live a healthy and productive lifestyle which takes into account their illness.

Cognitive Behavioural Therapy

CBT will not cure schizophrenia but it will help with many aspects of the illness:
- compliance with medication
- helping to recognise symptoms early
- working to prevent the faulty thinking patterns of depression
- working with the family prevent relapse & promotes calm

Pet Therapy

You may remember I mentioned pet therapy earlier. One of the symptoms of schizophrenia is the inability to gain pleasure out of doing things (anhedonia). It has been found that introducing patients to pets during therapy makes a considerable difference to this aspect of the illness. Pet therapy is relatively new, and not yet widely available but definitely worthwhile exploring.

Mental Illness & Social Exclusion

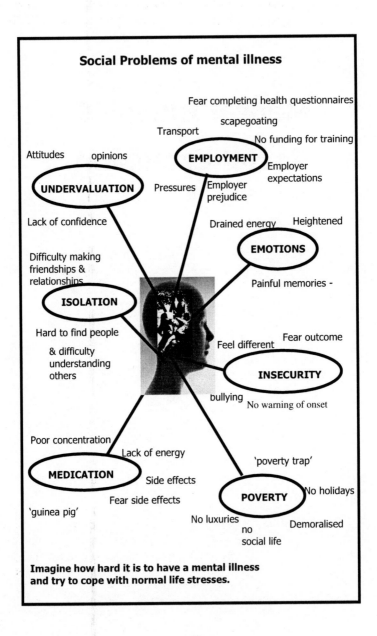

Social Problems of mental illness

Fear completing health questionnaires

scapegoating

Transport

No funding for training

Attitudes   opinions

EMPLOYMENT

Employer
expectations

UNDERVALUATION   Pressures   Employer
prejudice

Lack of confidence

Drained energy   Heightened

EMOTIONS

Difficulty making
friendships &
relationships

Painful memories -

ISOLATION

Hard to find people   Fear outcome

& difficulty   Feel different
understanding
others   **INSECURITY**

bullying   No warning of onset

Poor concentration

Lack of energy

'poverty trap'

MEDICATION   Side effects

No holidays

Fear side effects   **POVERTY**

'guinea pig'   No luxuries   Demoralised
no
social life

**Imagine how hard it is to have a mental illness
and try to cope with normal life stresses.**

"People who suffer from mental health problems remain one of the most excluded groups in society"
Rosie Winterton, Health Minister

CHAPTER 12

Stigma & Social Exclusion

This Chapter includes:

How Groups Operate
• Man, The Social Animal
• Why Social Inclusion Matters
• Why People Are Excluded
Why Stigmatisation?
• Physical Signs of Illness
• Appearance
• Sensational News Reports
• Mental Health Education
The Stigma of Diagnosis
Comparison Attitudes
Personal Effects of Exclusion
• Imagination Exercise
• Loneliness
• Worsening the Illness
• Low Self Esteem

Problems of Employability
• Lack of Work & Poverty
• Temporary Work
• Lack of Skills Training
• Voluntary Work
• Barriers to Employability
• Fear of Pressure at Work
• Fear of Misunderstanding
• Erratic Course of Mental Illness
• Barriers for Employers

By now, I hope you will have gained some insight into mental illness; its presumed causes, the raft of potential cures and how an individual might experience it. You know who the therapists are, how they work and the underpinning legislation. But is that the end of the story? Sadly not.

A man teaching a group of horticultural students with learning disabilities said, that although his students were ready for the community, the community was not yet ready for them. I think this applies to people with long term mental illness. The situation is improving with better communication, better media liaison and public education initiatives to tackle the problem head on, but we are not as far advanced as our neighbours in the USA. So what is stigma, where does it come from and how does it manifest? We need to understand:

- why humans tend to exclude others who are different
- why the stigma of mental illness breeds to social exclusion
- what happens when people are socially excluded

I will attempt to answer some of these questions in this chapter, but first let's look at how human beings operate in groups.

How Groups Operate - Inclusion & Exclusion

Man, the Social Animal

Man is a hunter gatherer by nature and a social animal. Thousands of years ago, he learned that group co-operation meant successful hunting and this in turn lead to a better chance of survival. The human being is programmed to survive.

There were inter-group rivalries no doubt and fights over mates - a trait shared with our animal past. Perhaps these natural rivalries sowed the seeds of later rejection of those who did belong - either to a perceived tribal group (or community), because they were rivals for scarce resources, or because they represented a threat to the group for other reasons.

Why Social Inclusion Matters

Imagine the circumstances of the early hunter-gatherers and the later farmers. Hunting in groups, or utilising the individual skills of your fellow tribe members in farming, early men started to find individual identity within a group. Once you have started this process the group and individuals benefit. The group as a whole becomes more successful because it contains experts who improve their skills and therefore obtain better results.

It does not matter what these skills are: potter, rope maker, shaman (magician or priest), plough-maker, maker of tools.

Individuals have some choice about their trade, can take pleasure in their creative skills and gain confidence. However, these conditions contain the seeds of vulnerability too.

What if the local expert leaves or dies or wanders off to another tribe. If the other members have forgotten how to make the right magic or make bronze tools; they are in danger from animals and other tribes. If an individual loses his broad range of skills through lack of practice he is vulnerable if rejected by the group.

Tribes lived in a highly fragile and hostile world. Under these circumstances, social inclusion was a matter of survival.

Why People Are Excluded

As far as the tribe or group is concerned, it is imperative they do not retain members who are likely to pose a threat to group survival. A tribal group will have leaders who are believed to be powerful magicians; those who direct the course of the tribe's life. If they dislike or fear someone and cannot be appeased that person is ultimately doomed. This might sound like many work places - you can now see its historic roots!

Human beings possess negative traits, as well as moral ones; envy, spite, fear, greed, suspicion, misunderstandings, a drive to destroy, fear of the unknown. These powerful feelings can lead to rejection of individuals who are perceived as different, cause fear, or are the targets of envy. Older members might fear being displaced, younger members want more power.

Personal self confidence can appear challenging in a group which is vulnerable, more so than in groups where individuals all have a sense of their own worth and environmental security. Such people will become targets for exclusion or assassination. So to sum up:

- confident groups and individuals are less likely to reject
- vulnerable groups and insecure individuals more so

These are the seeds of all kinds of group rivalries whether the excuses are religious, sporting, ethnicity, looks, disability or behavioural traits. Mental illness has become another means by which individuals can be targeted, blamed, feared and ultimately rejected. The real problem is not the illness itself, but how it is perceived.

Why Stigmatisation?

People fear mental illness for many reasons:

- patients can exhibit strange mannerisms, or look strange
- believe those with mental illness might kill or harm them or
- have a mistaken belief mental illness is infectious like a virus
- be too embarrassed to ask the facts about mental illness
- fear they have a mental health problem themselves

Physical Signs of Mental Illness

The symptoms of mental illness cannot be seen except through behaviour and emotions. Some people with chronic (long term) mental illness do sometimes behave or look strange, talking to themselves, dressing oddly, exhibiting tics (uncontrollable facial or bodily muscle spasms), shouting at no-one in particular (probably hearing voices).

Some of these strange mannerisms are due to the chemicals in the medication, for example long term psychiatric drugs can result in tongue and lip smacking (tardive dyskinesia) or shaking (Parkinsonism).

Appearance

Strange or old fashioned clothing is a hallmark if you have been in hospital for decades, often wearing communal clothing, are living on benefit, or your illness is chronic. Under these conditions you will not be fashion-conscious. Younger patients who may well love fashion but have no spare cash to indulge the purchase of clothing on a regular basis.

Sensational News Reports

Ignorance around the meaning of mental illness, around the facts of its control or cure is another reason for stigmatisation. Even in the 21st century with all the information we have thrown at us a huge proportion of the public only know what they know because of headlines like:

"Crazy axe murderer killer gets life" or "young actress in suicide bid" or "schizo gets life".

The media has been co-operating for years with mental health charities and Government to remove such headlines in favour of fact, less sensationalism, more explanation. Far more murders, as I have said, are committed by so-called sane people than by the mentally ill. And some so-called normal neighbours act in a disgusting way.

Mental Health Education

Mental health education initiatives are being started where they should have been years ago; in primary schools, in communities, in surgeries. Mental illness is being looked at from its more positive side - prevention. Mental health for everyone is now a Government priority, with recent figures showing mental illness and stress to be the number one reason for sickness absence in this country, a sobering thought.

The Stigma of Diagnosis

With a physical symptom, a general practitioner has physical clues to aid diagnosis. If a patient has a painful leg and has recently fallen whilst skiing, the G.P. notices bruising and swelling and concludes "You, sir, have a suspected fracture".

The patient, duly grateful, will comply by having an x-ray in a local hospital. Following this he will accept the usual treatment of plaster cast and physiotherapy. His relatives will usually be happy at the outcome and visit the hospital in droves. Mental illness diagnoses are more difficult to make and accept. The G.P. cannot look at his patient and say "You, sir, are mentally ill". The G.P. might be taken to court for defamation and the patient might not believe him. Relatives might be distressed or angry and embarrassed to visit psychiatric hospitals. So a kind of shamed isolation sets in which creates further stress for the unfortunate patient.

Patients with any kind of mental symptoms are likely to have no insight into the changes in their behaviour and can easily become angry or upset. Think of times you have been stressed and didn't realize how tetchy you had been until someone pointed it out.

Even in the 21st century, a diagnosis of mental illness is not as palatable as a physical disorder because of social stigma. There is an urban myth that mental illness is connected with moral or psychological weakness, which is of course absurd.

Attitudes to Mental & Physical Illnesses –

A Comparison

I hope you will see the absurdity of the difference in attitudes towards schizophrenia (or any major mental illness); and cancer, physical disability as in the table on the next page.

I have tried to demonstrate the different attitudes which result from different kinds of diagnoses. Some illnesses are perceived as sexy and glamorous in a morose kind of way, for example cancer or disfigurement. But mental illness is somehow seen to be the patient's fault, a result of being weak, morally degenerative, or somehow odd or scary. Someone with extensive scarring will be viewed with pity and compassion, whereas someone with OCD depression or schizophrenia might be shunned. It is a strange, illogical and totally mindless set of judgements being put into action, and hopefully ones which will disappear as time goes on.

SCHIZOPHRENIA or DEPRESSION	PATIENT WITH CANCER or a PHYSICAL DISABILITY
Perceived Causes: ♣ sign of 'weakness' ♣ 'no of emotional control'. ♣ Physical causes not seen ♣ suffering is patient's fault	**Perceived Causes:** ♣ possibly genetic factors ♣ physical cause - emotions seen as 'normal' response ♣ outside patient's control
community attitude to patient ♣ community message - patient responsible for their illness ♣ fear and distrust ♣ avoid - social exclusion ♣ stigmatised ♣ sense of disgust ♣ dangerous ♣ negative media image ♣ visitors ashamed to visit	**community attitude to patient** ♣ community raise funds for 'miracle' cures ♣ respect & admiration ♣ offer help and comfort ♣ 'heroic' perception ♣ sense of awe ♣ sympathy ♣ patient has many visitors

Personal Effects of Social Exclusion

Dumped in the Community

Long-term hospitalisation brings problems for those who need to move back into the community.

In institutions like hospitals there are regular offices of the day which are carried out at set times:

- waking, topping and tailing (toiletting & washing)
- drugs rounds
- organised activity such as occupational therapy
- meals
- therapy

Imagination Exercise

If you have been in hospital, remember how easy it seemed at first. Meals were ordered then arrived on a tray by your bed; friends popped in to pass time; the WRVS was only just down the corridor to provide extras. If you discount the incapacity which took you there, did you find it hard to pick up the threads of home life for the first few days?

Imagine you had been in hospital for most of your adult life. You quickly lose the ability to survive outside that situation. We have a word for this; institutionalisation. It happens very quickly to all sorts of people; fit young men in the forces, prisoners, highly intelligent people confined by totalitarian regimes; long standing social groups who resent outsiders.

People who have lived for years in highly organised and structured environments find it very difficult if not impossible to structure their day, no matter what their age, health state or disability.

If you experience constant audio or visual hallucinations it is hard enough to cope in hospital. With the added distractions of the outside world, forms, letters, bill payments, neighbour disputes and money, it becomes impossible. Being dumped in an uncaring community is a recipe for relapse.

Imagine you are an ex patient

You have been invited to a party and want to go as you are feeling lonely. As the day draws near, you start to get nervous:

- you don't know about fashion and you have no money for clothes. Will they make fun of you
- will they notice your hands shaking

- will they ask where you lived before - how will they react if you say a psychiatric hospital
- how do you make small talk; you have no history of living in the community
- will they spotlight you by talking about your illness
- what if you make a fool of yourself by making a mistake for example eating with the wrong implement

Would you still go to the party? If you didn't, how would you react next time someone asks? How are you going to relieve your loneliness?

It does not surprise me that places such as prisons may begin to look appealing. At least there is regularity, security, therapy, no one asks awkward questions, you don't have the nightmare of shopping and cooking and someone is always there to chat and relieve loneliness.

Loneliness

Community life is good for those good at socialising and joining in. Many patients with severe mental illness do not have these social skills; they have never learned them or at least forgotten how. On benefit, there is little left over for socialising even going to a cinema (although urban myth will tell you differently).

Worsening the Illness

Peace of mind, one of the best interventions for mental trauma, is hard to find in modern life. If you add coping with stigma; jeering youths, gossipy neighbours, people who won't talk to anyone remotely different, then anyone might start to feel ill.

Medication is easy to forget unless there someone on hand to remind. Sometimes it is hard to remember, sometimes the side effects are so bad no one would want to take it. Sometimes there is so much distraction from hallucinations that patients are not aware of what day it is let alone when they last took medication. Under these conditions there is bound to be relapse.

Low Self Esteem

Having read so far you may realize that people with mental illness often undervalue themselves. To undervalue yourself is to reduce your human potential. No one with low self esteem is likely to enhance their skills and gifts. I have seen this in the faces of many people I met during my career; 'if only I had not had this illness...' what then.

Having the illness is sad enough but not having opportunities to make some kind of life with some human happiness is a tragedy.

Problems of Employability

Lack of Work & Resulting Poverty

A survey carried out in 2001 by Focus found seventy five percent of people with mental illness considered they were on a low income and led a frills free, isolated existence. For people who have to exist on benefits, poverty is a lasting problem.

Those who hold down jobs are luckier but a large proportion of the population with long periods of mental illness are not working in jobs which reflect their academic ability, creativity or other skills. One reason might be the huge amounts of energy lost that could have been channelled into climbing the career ladder.

The Problem With Temporary Work

People with mental illness might come to the career market late in life if at all. If they lack the confidence or have a CV with long periods of unemployment they could easily fall into the temporary work trap. Many agencies offer this kind of commercial work which commands high fees from their corporate clients but pays below the market rate for the job. They call this cheap labour 'flexible work' or 'contracting' or 'getting back into the labour market'. There are few employment laws in temporary work. Billions of pounds per year are being earned through this most profitable of human traffic.

Lack of Skills Training

Huxley commented with black humour that funding agencies in his day existed to prevent those who need the money most from getting it. The situation has not changed much. It is a fact that no one on benefits can afford to pay thousands of pounds to complete a decent training course.

I wonder if it has changed much in effect since George Orwell *wrote* 'Down and Out in London and Paris' or 'The Road to Wigan Pier'. This is human garbage; intelligence left to rot in grubby towns and dingy bedsits throughout the country and I can only hope that changes in the form of real opportunities and solid funding appear in my lifetime. I doubt it.

Voluntary Work

Many people take on voluntary work as a means of motivation and ego building, but it does not resolve the basic means problem although it does provide a measure of self esteem and practice in social skills building. However, it is unfair to expect voluntary jobs to be filled by people with disabilities.

Voluntary work is not going to resolve the wider issues of psychological well being and acceptance which only come through living and working with others in the wider community and being paid the going rate. Mental health charities are just getting wise to this and starting to demand better conditions for their members.

Barriers to Employability

There are barriers from the job seeker's point of view and there are barriers from employers point of view. If someone does not have professional qualifications they are likely to stay in the poverty trap unless they are artistically successful or turn to crime. People with mental illness are competing against others who are not so disadvantaged.

Perhaps, like a man I know with an IQ of Mensa level, they might be offered a job as a cleaner on a Government sponsored scheme.

Many people, even professionals, tend to forget the intellectual ability trapped inside symptoms which label a man or a woman 'a depressive' or 'a schizo' or someone with autism.

Fear of Pressure at Work

There will be times when someone with mental illness needs time off work; but on the other hand a so-called normal person will need time off too. Real structures need to be in place to ensure support by the occupational health system.

Anyone who has been out of work for a lengthy period will experience the same anxieties about coping as someone with mental illness. In most companies there is more work than there are man-hours as a result of cost-cutting which results in considerable stress for all staff. This can pile on the stress for someone with an existing mental health problem.

Fear of Misunderstanding

The existing workforce is not different from the rest of society as regards education around mental illness. This is hugely surprising given that 1:4 people will undergo mental illness. This could be resolved by providing mental health education at an early stage in life, a task the Government has recently started to undertake on a large scale. Fear of being ostracised at work is a real issue. Bullying is common in the workplace (current estimates 25%). People with mental illnesses are obvious targets with emotional insecurities, strange behaviours or lack of street wisdom. No one wants to go out to work and find they are in a worse state of mental health than before they went.

The Erratic Course of Mental Illness

Staff can consult DSMIV (diagnostics and statistics manual), perhaps thanks to brain scanning they might be able to point with accuracy to where brain chemistry is causing a problem. They might, thanks to the unravelling of the human genome (DNA sequence) be able to give you the number of the sequence or the name of the hormone causing the problem. What they cannot yet do is say <u>when</u> you are likely to experience an episode of mental illness or <u>how</u> you will experience it (in emotional or behavioural terms).

The erratic course of mental illness, and inability to predict when episodes might occur, make employment more hazardous outside social enterprises. However, if you look at the figures for sickness and stress the same could be said for any employee.

Barriers for Employers

Barriers exist on the other side too; that of potential employers. There is the same question about the unknown quantity. Employers need to consider existing staff reactions to new colleagues. It can be, as my friend commented, like putting a giraffe in a herd of elephants.

Within the creative industry there is more tolerance otherwise you would not have been able to enjoy the talents of DJ Kenny Everett or actor Jeremy Brett, both of whom had well publicised mental illness.

These are by no means all the reasons why mentally ill patients are social excluded whether they have long term episodic illness or a one-off attack. But what are we doing about this?

"All persons with mental illness... shall be treated with humanity and respect...."
United Nations Resolution, December 1991

Chapter 13

Improving Social Inclusion

This Chapter Contains:

Who is Responsible for Social Exclusion
Changing The Language
• [Imagination exercise]
What Can Be Done to Improve Social Inclusion?
• [Imagination exercise]
Meaningful work
The Problem With Mental Health Clubs

Who is Responsible for Social Exclusion

The answer to this question is, everyone. We all have some kind of prejudice, whether or not we admit it. Prejudice comes from many sources:

• schools (copied attitudes)
• family attitudes (what is learned in the early years)
• communities (peer pressure is very strong)
• faith organisations
• work colleagues
• what is seen in the media - a powerful attitude former

As you read in the previous chapter, man is a social being, but at the time suspicious of anyone who is different and might threaten group security. However, as the only animals with consciousness, that is the ability to think (awareness), man is equipped to learn and change. And learning and changing is what social inclusion is all about. So, let's change the word 'exclusion' for 'inclusion', be more positive and see what we can all do to improve matters.

Changing The Language

The language of stigma is negative, breeds contempt, mistrust, ridicule.

☞ **Imagine you have a serious mental illness (manic depressive psychosis)**

Your name is Jo[e] Smith. You live in a small town. You have manic depressive psychosis. You work as an artist.

Which of these would you **really like** to hear about yourself?

crazy	Mr[s] Smith is artistic
mental	looney
Jo[e] is kind	Jo[e]'s on a high again
misery guts	Jo[e]'s moody again
my neighbour	Jo[e] is unwell at the moment
he's depressive	I love Jo[e]'s art
nutter	oddball
that oddball	Jo[e] makes me laugh
my colleague	Jo[e] has manic depression
psycho	Jo[e]'s mental
nuts	Jo[e] is my friend
bananas	Joe, the artist

Words do matter very much so don't let anyone convince you otherwise. People with mental illness are people, not the other way around. They are neighbours, friends, relatives, confidantes, colleagues; part of the same community you live in.

What Can Be Done to Improve Social Inclusion?

Everyone can do something, absolutely everyone. In the following section, try to think what you could do to improve your community by reducing stigma. You don't need vast resources, high intellect, just the will to try and patience to continue even if it does not appear to work at first.

'How Can I Help Improve Social Inclusion'?

Social inclusion is not about someone else doing something, it is YOU. This is challenging for you. If you come up with ideas contact me via the publisher and I will include the best in the next version of this book - and your name if you want.

I have included some ideas in the boxes which follow - I challenge you to try one for yourself OR think up your own AND ACT UPON IT.

Professionals

put up posters in public places

give talks to the community

offer company stress courses

organise green gyms

put books in libraries

ditto, in mobile libraries

Survivors & Patients

record your story - you are a living resource

be open about your illness

challenge negative language

write letters to the local rag when you hear something negative

challenge inequality

join community activities

Government

use NI payments to fund sickness periods

put funding into small initiatives

ministers reveal own mental illness

appoint service users to PCT's

make time to debate social inclusion

promote mental health at every opportunity

Organisations / Companies

think twice before rejecting someone with mental illness

fit the person to the job, rather than the other way around

encourage employees to attend stress courses

hold mental health surgeries

put up posters about social inclusion

encourage employees to report bullying

The Media

publish reports of recovery

publish features on mental health

offer prizes for community initiatives

encourage readers to promote mental health

initiate community projects

encourage readers through competitions

Community Organisations

make sure all your programmes are inclusive

act as befriender to those new to the community

put up posters

offer transport

ask local mental health services to provide speakers

provide free courses for those on benefit, without making it obvious

Meaningful work

In the Asylums there were workshops where in-patients would spend the whole working day putting together parts for manufacturers. The workshops were run on production lines like mini factories. They filled a gap but were drab and uninspiring places to spend a day. For work to be meaningful in any sense, it has to fulfil three functions:

- to provide a genuine end product
- to provide a sense of fulfilment and achievement
- to provide a sense of belonging (sense of identity)

There are some excellent co-operatives in which the businesses (such as shops and small enterprises) are run by the workers

195

themselves. Chipmunka is a social enterprise publishing narrative (personal experiences of mental illness). There is no reason why such schemes should not be run by patients of mental health services. Funding is available for such schemes.

Employers need to be less afraid, and far more aware, of the provision of decent work for people with mental health problems and to reduce sickness due to stress at work. Stress is on the same continuum as mental illness so this is a real wake-up call.

The Problem with Mental Health Clubs

In mental health clubs it is easier for patients who understand each other to socialise together. They do not have to undergo the trauma of going to venues where people might not be accepting. They also offer some respite to carers.

However, this sort of community resource could unwittingly help create mental health ghettos. Patients who later recover or those with episodic mental illness could be trapped, not having the confidence to leave a supportive mental health user club to try their luck in the open community.

There are many good things about day centres and clubs, especially for those unlikely to recover. When the community is ready to provide social inclusion for everyone, they will have outlived their usefulness.

Mental Health & the Law

"Even when I have been most psychotic– I have been aware of finding new corners in my mind and heart"
Dr Kay Redfield Jamison 'An Unquiet Mind'

Chapter 14
The Mental Health Act 1983

The Contents of this Chapter:
Definitions of Professionals within the 1983 Act
Sections of the 1983 Act
Applications for Sections
Epilogue

When you read this chapter, try to remember Kay Jamison's words (above). Even if someone becomes psychotic that doesn't mean they lose their humanity. They are still daughter, brother, mother, father, friend, uncle, colleague. Forced hospitalisation and treatment is, in most cases, temporary and patients will eventually return to their lives in the community.

The stated aim of the current Act is *"the reception, care and treatment of mentally disordered patients, the management of their property and other related matters"*. This is the legal machinery by which those are considered a danger to themselves or the public can be treated.

The Act is divided into sections. The term sectioning describes how someone is taken into care e.g. "(s)he was sectioned". Each section covers a specific area.

Definitions of Professionals Within the 1983 Act

The Act specifies responsibilities of the mental health workers and I will identify the major players.

Approved Social Worker (ASW)

A qualified social worker who has taken special training to make applications for committing an unwell person to hospital.

Mental Health Review Tribunal (MHRT)

The MHRT consists of professional and non professional members. Tribunals are appointed by the Lord Chancellor. They are legal bodies.

Nearest Relative

The nearest relative means a close relative of the patient (spouse, partner, parent). If this relative is a spouse they must be married to the patient or have been living with the patient for at least 6 months.

In the case of gay partners, they must have lived as partners for at least 5 years. The person must be over 18 years. If no relative exists the Courts can appoint someone to act on the patient's behalf.

Responsible Medical Officer (RMO)

RMO is the person responsible for the medical care of the patient in hospital; usually the psychiatrist treating the patient.

Sections of the 1983 Act

As you read these imagine yourself or a relative being sectioned. Consider your vulnerability. Clinicians and Tribunals will be making decisions which have serious consequences for your future social standing and career. Your letters might be opened. You are not allowed to walk in hospital gardens. Think what it feels like to be imprisoned against your will - do you feel angry or helpless?

Once a patient has been detained in psychiatric hospital for a long time, there is a danger of institutionalisation. After weeks or months of being cared for, people lose the will and social skills to live outside the confines of a hospital.

Applications for Sections

Applications have to be made for all sections of the Act. These are formal papers which legally enable someone to be admitted to Hospital for treatment even if they do not wish to go. Applications have to be made by:

- an Approved Social Worker who has seen the person within the previous 14 days
- qualified doctors of medicine or psychiatry

Section 2 – Admission for Assessment
Used for:
- persons not admitted before
- existing patients of mental health service
- on application from 2 medical recommendations
- detention for up to 28 days
- grounds for sectioning–a severe mental disorder which needs assessment and it is in his/her safety or safety of the public

Two doctors may detain for 28 days under this section. This is a long time for someone to be in a psychiatric hospital, especially if it is the first time.

Can you imagine how anxiety provoking this might be? How would you cope with living for 28 days in the presence of severely mentally ill people especially if you are unused to bizarre behaviour and strongly expressed emotions? Would your family and friends visit, or would they be too embarrassed?

Section 3 – Admission for Treatment

- application by 2 medical referees
- can be admitted for up to 6 months
- can be renewed for 6 months on first application, then a year on all subsequent applications
- grounds - interests of patient safety or protection of the public

This section is those who have been committed under Section 2 and allows extra time for treatment to take place. It cannot be imposed if the patient's nearest relative objects (under this Act).

Would you consider you had enough experience to oppose a decision made by a Mental Health professional? Would you feel responsible?

Section 4 – Emergency admission

- only used in cases of emergency
- application by 1 medical referee
- can be admitted for up to 72 hours (3 days)
- grounds; severe mental illness; unsafe for the patient or public for him/her to be left at large

This section needs the agreement of only one medical referee.

What if the doctor is tired, does not know you and has to make a decision in a hurry. The person to be admitted might be of a different culture or naturally lively or aggressive. Might this colour the doctor's opinion? Remember these are decisions which will affect that person's future.

Section 20 – Renewal (of a Section)

This section is applied if:

- the renewal of an existing section for 6 months (1st), then 1 year periods thereafter
- the patient will improve or not deteriorate if given treatment the renewal is for the safety of the patient or the public
- Mental Health Managers have to review the patient

  Mental Health Managers are members of the Mental Health Trust Board with varying degrees of experience in mental health. These renewals are 6 months to one year's detention in hospital.

Imagine how a new patient might be affected being with seriously ill patients during the period of admission.

Section 23 – Discharge

- used before the end of a section when it is considered the patient is fit to be discharged
- the Nearest Relative can request an early discharge
- Mental Health Review Tribunal can overrule discharge if the patient is considered dangerous
- a patient can remain in hospital voluntarily even if discharged

The procedure for discharge is lengthy and involves a Tribunal (a panel of experts and lay people appointed by the Lord Chancellor).

Relatives have some say but can be overruled by the Medical Referee or Tribunal.

☝ Might mental health workers look for signs of illness. Would misinterpretations of behaviour or speech be possible? Might patients be afraid to face the real world and therefore have a vested interest in remaining sectioned? Would relatives want to discharge ill patients for their own reasons?

Sections 57 Consent to Treatment

This Section is for consent to treatment with psycho surgery or hormonal implants

- for a patient who has given voluntary consent
- the treatment must cure or alleviate the patient's condition
- 3 medical persons must confirm that the patient understands the nature of the treatment

Psycho surgery includes lobotomy, now rarely performed. It involves detaching the frontal lobes of the brain in order to modify behaviour. Such surgery had devastating effects on the person's intellect and mood.

☝ Does consent mean that doctor or patient will be fully aware of implications? What is the alternative for the patient and the public if the surgery is denied?

Section 58 Consent to Treatment (with a second opinion)

This section is for consent to treatment by medication or ECT (electro convulsive therapy), for patients who:

- understand what the treatment involves
- have not given permission for the treatment*

- who are not likely to understand the nature and duration of the treatment*

* In these cases, the Mental Health Act Commission appoints a second opinion doctor who has to confirm that treatment will be beneficial, even if the patient refuses permission for treatment.

ECT is now highly regulated by NICE and can only be performed under strict conditions.

Section 93 Management of Financial Affairs

The gist of these sections are:

- medical evidence of mental illness is a prerequisite
- a person can be appointed by a Court of Protection with Power of Attorney*

  i.e. they are given legal permission to manage the finances of any person with severe mental illness (not necessarily a patient)

In all cases the person appointed has to keep financial records and report to the Court. They are required to act in the best interests of the patient.

 Imagine you are mentally ill but have flashes of awareness. During this time you realize someone else is looking after your finances. Would that make you feel vulnerable? Or would it be easier to let someone else take responsibility for you? What about when you are no longer ill - would you feel insecure?

Section 134 – Withholding of Correspondence

This section includes:

- the right to open or withhold patients outgoing mail if the addressee does not wish to receive such mail

- ditto, if it is felt* this mail will cause distress to the addressee
- right to withhold incoming mail* in the interests of patient or others safety

by the Mental Health Act Managers (MHAM)

Strict records have to be kept about withheld mail. Any mail addressed to MP's or legal advisers has to be delivered, unless they give written confirmation that mail is unwanted. This retains the right of the person in hospital to contact public figures. The patient can appeal to the Mental Health Act Commission for restoration of mail delivery, except where the addressee has written that they do not wish to receive such mail.

 Vetting incoming mail being stopped sounds totalitarian; but what if the patient in their delusion is seeking bomb making equipment or guns or knives? Manic patients might send letters with outrageous sexual suggestions or personal remarks. The recipient could be embarrassed, angry or inconvenienced. In these circumstances what is your opinion about the Royal Mail's duty to accept and deliver mail? Would you want such mail?

Section 135 – Power to Enter (Private) premises

- a warrant has to be obtained from a Justice of the Peace
- police officers can enter the premises by force
- a police officer, ASW and doctor must be present
- the person inside can be taken into a place of safety
- they can be kept for up to 72 hours (3 days)

The purpose of this section is to deal with persons who are in private premises and are believed to need urgent treatment for mental illness.

Imagine you are in a safe place or your own home. You are

taken from there forcibly, perhaps with neighbours looking on, and driven to a strange building. You don't realize what is happening or what to expect. Would you feel frightened?

Families may have had to wait for a considerable time for a section to be made. Imagine living in the same house as someone behaving in a bizarre way especially for lengthy periods of time.

Section 136 – Removal of People from Public Places

- a police officer can remove anyone from a public area for mental health assessment
- they can be kept in a place of safety for up to 72 hours (3 days)

This is a very controversial section. In multi-cultural communities there can be misinterpretation of behaviour. Police officers are not trained mental health workers although some Health Authorities and Trusts provide short courses for them.

Epilogue

I hope this chapter has given you some food for thought. Human rights have to be balanced with public safety. This is becoming more difficult at a time when everyone wants to assert their rights. There are no easy answers but I hope you now have a clearer idea of some of the many issues and considerations involved.

"The Bill [in wider context of mental health reform] aims to ... help people with a mental disorder early enough so that fewer people reach crisis level."
Rosie Winterton (Minister for Health)

Chapter 15

The Mental Health Bill 2004

This chapter contains:
Why New Legislation Is Required
The Mental Health Bill 2004
The New Bill - Flowchart
Conditions for the Legislation to be applied (Department of Health Directive)
What People Fear Generally
Issues about the Bill from Mind (a major Mental Health Charity)
The Government's Answers to Questions About the Legislation
Department Of Health On How Patients Will Benefit From The Bill
How the Bill Has Been Developed Since 2002
How A Bill Becomes Law
Implementation of Bill
July 2005 Progress
Other Legislation Which Impacts on the Mental Health Bill
Information from Department of Health Websites (in this chapter)

The proposed Bill has been discarded following a storm of protest by individuals and mental health charities. However, I feel it important for students of mental illness to understand the process, and have therefore left this chapter in.

This chapter is slightly different to the last. Rather than setting imagination exercises, I have extracted the bare facts from a variety of interesting sources and included where possible the Government's wording.

 As you read this chapter:

✤ consider the moral issues - remember, the balances are: care for the patient, the safety of the public (human rights issues)

✤ the need to change the law in the light of better medications and community treatment

✤ the fact that the Government are now committing millions of pounds for community services to treat mentally ill patients and reduce social exclusion

 Try to put yourself in all these roles in turn:

👊 patient
👊 member of the public
👊 clinician
👊 mental health charity worker
👊 carer

Why New Legislation Is Required

The modern pattern of community care and the rise of effective treatments have gradually changed the environment in which the Mental Health Act 1983 is operating. There are far more services available for patients with serious mental illnesses outside hospitals, for example:

- assertive outreach
- crisis resolution
- home treatment
- early intervention for psychosis

Civil liberties are far more an issue and European Law has to be taken into account. However, that has to be balanced with public anxiety about safety (albeit the number of patients with serious personality disorders who are considered a public danger is minimal). This Bill represents new legislation "*to improve the provision of mental health services and make them more focused on the needs of the individual*" (Department of Health).

The Mental Health Bill 2004 proposals have been the cause of anxieties expressed by mental health charities, which fear the erosion of civil liberties among those mentally ill patients who are not, and never have been, a danger to the public. Some of these concerns are listed later in this chapter [thanks to Mind for providing a summary of the points for me).

Finally, the 1983 Act itself is imprecise and needs to be clarified, for example the reason for detention on grounds of patient safety read 'for the health or safety of the patient'. This is open to all sorts of interpretation, and the new Bill provides for the more structured " for the protection of the patient from suicide or serious self-harm or serious neglect by him of his health or safety'.

The Mental Health Bill 2004

There are 3 parts to the proposed bill the first of which explains the provisions. Part two is concerned with how civil procedures are conducted and part three about entry to the act through the criminal justice system.

The Government's aims for the Bill are that it:

- 'defines clear and fair procedures for assessment and treatment. There will be a new Tribunal system that will authorise use of formal powers beyond the initial assessment of the patient'
- 'provides a number of safeguards to ensure good decision-making, including the involvement of service users and their representatives. The system will be independently inspected'
- 'ensures there is support for patients so that their voice is heard' [quotations from Department of Health].

The New Bill - Flowchart

I have simplified the following flowchart from the Department of Health's publication. It shows the process from reporting of an incident of need to admission.

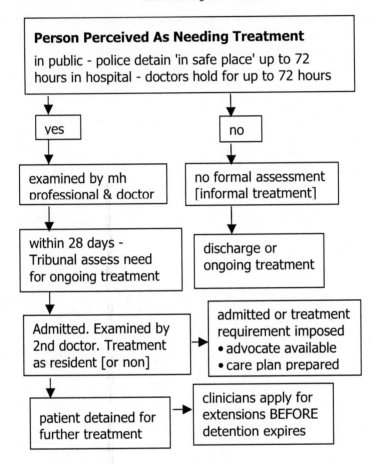

Person Perceived As Needing Treatment

in public - police detain 'in safe place' up to 72 hours in hospital - doctors hold for up to 72 hours

yes → examined by mh professional & doctor → within 28 days - Tribunal assess need for ongoing treatment → Admitted. Examined by 2nd doctor. Treatment as resident [or non] → patient detained for further treatment

no → no formal assessment [informal treatment] → discharge or ongoing treatment

admitted or treatment requirement imposed
• advocate available
• care plan prepared

clinicians apply for extensions BEFORE detention expires

Conditions for the Legislation to be applied (Department of Health Directive)

- a person must be suffering from 'a mental disorder of such a nature or degree as to warrant the provision of treatment under the supervision of a specialist doctor or senior mental health practitioner'

- treatment must be 'necessary for the protection of the patient from suicide, serious self-harm or serious neglect of their health or safety, or for the protection of others'

- only if 'appropriate treatment cannot be provided unless the powers in the Bill are used (except for patients over 16 at substantial risk of causing serious harm to others)'
- appropriate treatment must actually be available

What People Fear Generally

- the Bill is a means of control for those considered a danger to society and they will be subjected to forcible treatment
- forced detention of unconventional or eccentric people
- indefinite detention
- forcible treatment in the community
- clinicians fear becoming prison officers in the community
- clinicians fear Tribunals will be able to detain without consultation with them

A Summary of Mind's Proposals For A New Act

(this list was kindly provided by Mind)

- that general principles should be on the face of the Act
- that the Code of Practice should have mandatory status
- that there should be narrower conditions for the exercise of compulsory powers – in particular removing the possibility of using compulsory powers on people with full decision-making capacity and retaining a test of therapeutic benefit.
- no compulsion in the community
- improved safeguards for advocates and nominated persons
- statutory recognition of the role of advance statements
- a reconstitution of the tribunal to include a role for non-medical members and service users
- an improved duty to provide aftercare
- a removal of the police power to enter private premises without a warrant
- the right of accused persons to the same safeguards (nominated person, Tribunal) as for civil patients
- a complete prohibition on the administration of ECT on all patients who have capacity and who have refused treatment, and (except for saving life) on all patients without capacity.
- legally binding safeguards to protect people from potentially

hazardous practices, including a specific requirement that doses above British National Formulary [the manual which limits the dosage of medications] limits should not be given without informed consent."

The Government's Response to Public Questions About the Legislation

General

➢ dangerous patients do not have the choice of 'voluntary' treatment in the community. They can be detained for up to 28 days for assessment but further detention must be decided by a Tribunal. They can be forced to accept treatment in hospital but not in the community

➢ patient and their families/carers will have access to independent advocates

➢ nurses and clinicians with appropriate skills & training will be able to take on statutory roles which were the preserve of e.g. Approved Social Workers for example: clinical supervisors, clinical members of Tribunals, approved mental health professionals

On Detention

➢ the legal right to detain people who need treatment has existed since 1959. The Bill provides for people <u>who can be,</u> to be treated in the community e.g. existing patients known to the services. New patients will be detained in hospital for assessment first before being given treatment in the community

➢ no one can be detained under the new Bill unless they have a recognised mental disorder, there is evidence of danger to the public, suicide, self harm, or neglect, AND that there is relevant suitable treatment available

➢ clinical and social care [Social Services] staff will decide if all conditions for compulsive detention exist, including suitable treatment - if not, a patient cannot be detained

➢ Tribunals discretionary powers to detain will be limited to dangerously mentally disordered persons [DSPD]

On Treatment

➢ treatment is **not** at home but is subject to requirements e.g. attending an outpatient clinic weekly. If a detained patient fail to do this, they can be required to become a resident patient

➢ The programme dealing with people considered dangerous (Dangerous and Severe Personality Disordered or DSPD) is happening under the current [1983] Act

➢ mentally disordered offenders who are not a danger allowed treatment in the community instead of prison

➢ courts given enhanced powers to make decisions about treatment i.e. offset criminalization of minor offenders with mental health problems by imposing mental health order instead of prison

Department Of Health
On How Patients Will Benefit From The Bill

• everyone will have a representative & advocate
• Tribunal has to assess need for detention after 28 days
• healthcare Commission assesses standards of care
• families & carers [where appropriate] regularly updated about patient's treatment
• 'harm to self' now has higher threshold - i.e. risk of suicide, self harm, neglect
• in order for someone to be detained, suitable treatment MUST be available
• individual care plans; to be approved by Tribunal or a Court
• some patients can be treated in the community - NOT potentially dangerous patients
• patients detained have right to be involved in decisions about their care & can refuse ECT

- patients can nominate someone to represent their views
- patients apply direct to the Tribunal for discharge
- minor criminal offenders given the opportunity of being treated in hospital or community instead of prison
- detained patients will have a nominated person to be appointed as their clinical supervisor
- detentions are 28 days, 6 months, a further 2 x 6 months, then 1 year intervals

How the Bill Developed Since 2002

better definition of 'mental disorder'	definition tightened to show the psychological effect [rather than the cause]
detention of patient for their health and safety [too broad a brush]	Now "protection of the patient from suicide or serious self-harm or serious neglect by him of his health or safety".
available treatments	holistic approach
people eligible for formal powers - i.e. treatment in the community	primarily 'known' patients. i.e. new patients need to have had a hospital assessment on a previous occasion
Tribunals will have over-riding powers of detention i.e. clinicians have little say	Tribunals' power limited to defined patients, who pose a definite risk to the community
	i.e. this is an exceptional condition not the norm
compulsory treatment in	Govt is no longer pursuing

prisons	this; recognises that prison is not an appropriate place for treatment
ECT	patients who are mentally capable can refuse this, 'except in emergency cases'.
healthcare commission to inspect hospitals where problems are reported	will also make ad hoc inspection visits
ill treatment by staff of patients - max sentence of 2 years is not enough	maximum prison sentence of 5 years to be instated
definition of 'carer'	implemented a wide definition of carer
patients agreement required before professionals can consult with them	patients wishes taken into consideration but clinicians need to consider consulting with carers

How a Bill Becomes Law

I thought readers might be interested in this process. This applies to any law.

The House of Commons Readings

- Introduction of material to House of Commons
- 2nd reading in House of Commons - and debate
- Commons Committee stage; detailed scrutiny of Bill, clause by clause
- Commons Report Stage; further debate on any amendments
- Commons 3rd reading - decision about the Bill as a whole

The House of Lords Readings

- Introduction of material to House of Lords and 1st reading
- House of Lords 2nd reading - and debate
- House of Lords Committee stage; detailed scrutiny of Bill, clause by clause
- House of Lords Report Stage; further debate
- House of Lords 3rd reading; further amendments

Inter-House of Readings

- House of Commons; House of Lords amendments
- Bill goes to and from House of Lords and Commons until Bill is agreed

The Legislation Stage

- Royal Assent is given and the Bill becomes an Act
- Act commences no less than 2 months later

Implementation (from the Department of Health)

In July 2005, the Implementation Group met to discuss the practical issues of implementation:

- mapping of the elements of workforce needed to implement Bill
- need to involve carers in implementation plans
- Reciprocity and aftercare
- the role of carers and their rights versus the rights of the nominated person
- the need for carers to be able to access the right type of care when needed
- Tribunals

The Bill allows staff with the right skills and experience to carry out key roles instead of restricting roles automatically to particular professional groups. A code of practice will be drawn up for patients, clinicians, hospital managers, tribunals. ASW's must to be approved as Approved Mental Health Professionals (they will be re-assessed) but are expected to be the mainstays for this role.

Letters have been sent by the Department of Health to all staff involved to explain how the Bill affects their roles. Finally, the implementation processes and support structures will be put in place.

Progress to July 2005

The Government has accepted over half of the Committee's 107 recommendations to date e.g.

- **The guiding principles will appear on the Bill**. - these apply to all the Bill's provisions and will help awareness and reduce stigma.

- **An exclusion for substance dependency.** This means clinicians will not be able to compulsorily treat people whose sole mental disorder is dependency on drugs or alcohol.

- **Improvements in patient rights** for example advance decisions and statements, Tribunal involvement in psychosurgery, patients' rights to decide whether advocates can see their records and patients meeting with advocates in private.

- **Improved rights for victims of mentally disordered offenders.** More consideration is to be given to victims' evidence statements when a court or tribunal is considering how to deal with mentally disordered offenders.

Other Legislation Which Impacts on the Bill

- Mental Capacity Bill
- Domestic Violence, Crime and Victims Bill

You can of course download all the documents, arguments and counter-arguments from the websites of the Department of Health and any of the major mental health charity websites.

Information from Department of Health Websites (in this chapter)

In accordance with my license to publish this material, these are the source websites:

Background to the Mental Health Bill 2004

http://www.dh.gov.uk/PolicyAndGuidance/HealthAndSocialCare Topics/MentalHealth/MentalHealthArticle/fs/en?CONTENT_ID =4089588&chk=we/GKL

Government's answers to fears about the proposed Mental Health Bill

http://www.dh.gov.uk/PolicyAndGuidance/HealthAndSocialCare Topics/MentalHealth/MentalHealthArticle/fs/en?CONTENT_ID =4089590&chk=LmO2JW

DH - How Patients will benefit from the Bill

http://www.dh.gov.uk/PolicyAndGuidance/HealthAndSocialCare Topics/MentalHealth/MentalHealthArticle/fs/en?CONTENT_ID =4089589&chk=1fWV90

July 2005 Mental Health Bill Implementation Group
http://www.dh.gov.uk/PolicyAndGuidance/HealthAndSocialCare Topics/MentalHealth/MentalHealthArticle/fs/en?CONTENT_ID =4121439&chk=NQAbet

Latest on Mental Health Bill

Government Report: 2005/0244

Organisations & Projects

'Health is defined in WHO's Constitution as 'a state of complete physical, mental and social well-being and not merely the absence of disease or infirmity'
World Health Organisation, Project Atlas Report

Chapter 16

World Health Organisation (WHO)

This Chapter contains:
World Resources
What is the World Health Organisation
The Mission of the World Health Organisation
World Health Report 2006
Project Atlas

World Resources

I would like to make a small point before we continue about the constant harping-on around lack of personnel and resources in the NHS. In 2005 in the UK (population 60 million) there were **2004** consultant generalist psychiatrists and **521** consultant old age psychiatrists (total **2525**). Remember, these are CONSULTANT grade so there are hundreds junior grades below them (new figures due May 2006).

In the Congo, one of the most deprived countries on earth, population 2.5 million there is **one** (total) psychiatrist. If you do the maths for this the number of consultant grade psychiatrists alone should be slightly over 100. Yet, read this man's story and it is very humbling:

http://www.who.int/healthsystems/psychiatrist/en/index.html

In an earlier chapter, I discussed that making a difference does not mean hurling money and resources at a project but looking at what resources exist and re-deploying those. It is something the armed forces, and also some voluntary and local organisations are very good at but has yet to be deployed more widely in the NHS.

What is the World Health Organisation

The World Health Organisation (WHO) is a specialist section of the United Nations, set up in 1948. Its headquarters is in Geneva and there are six regional offices across the globe staffed by health professionals and experts. The aim of WHO is to enable *"complete physical, mental and social well-being"* which *encompasses a holistic way of looking at health."*

WHO has six aims:

1. ethical health policy-making, based on clinical evidence
2. programmes of research
3. providing policies & programmes acceptable to member states
4. maintaining workable relationships with member states
5. responsibility for conception, implementation and follow-through of all new health standards
6. gathering data on new technology and improvements to health care

The Mission of the World Health Organisation

WHO mission is to *"clos*[e] *the gap between what is needed and what is currently available to reduce the burden of mental disorders world-wide, and promot*[e] *mental health"*.

World Health Report 2006

The World Health Organisation has a global remit to improve the health of all citizens world wide and is about to publish its World Health Report 2006 (April 2006). This includes a register of all services, resources and numbers of health care workers in place globally. Chief among the findings of WHO is that, in successfully meeting mental health project targets, the following factors have to be taken into account:

1. training a specialist health-care workforce to increase health

and health awareness
2. good organisation and the support of the workforce
3. the vital necessity of good leadership (governance or management) and stewardship (best use of resources)
4. international investment in the programme

Project Atlas

➢ Contributing to the above report was Project Atlas which I mentioned in the last edition. Readers will be interested to learn this massive project has now been successfully completed. I have included details of their website in the information section.

The value of having these figures publicly available is enormous; the pride factor for those governments with minimal funding making best use of resources. This must outweigh the 'name and shame' factor implied in the map, showing areas where no services or policies exist. As time goes on these gaps will become more blindingly obvious and open to world wide scrutiny.

Countries struggling to implement programmes in the face of financial limitations will be proud of their co-operation in this massive undertaking. The difficulties in obtaining statistics, the bias factor (where government statistics alone are currently relied upon) and the problems of ensuring a common language are gradually being resolved as the project proceeds.

Project Atlas will be a continuous project, but with improved global communications and the development of improved statistical measures the information will become more refined as time goes on. This is a valuable resource in the fight against mental health ignorance.

****

Well, having looked at the global picture, time for a brief venture into a very controversial area of mental health treatment. If any organisations could represent the scapegoats of the field, then it must be the giant pharmaceutical companies. Money-making machines or vital factors in the development of research and new treatments for mental illness? Judge for yourself in the next chapter.

"The Physiome Project is more than science: it is education, exploration, .. disseminating..databasing"
The Physiome Project

Chapter 17

Not Just the 'Big Bad Wolf' - Pharmaceuticals

New Drugs & Virtual Drug Trials

Contents of this Chapter:
The Necessity of Psychiatric Drugs
The Wonders of Science
Designing and Marketing New Drugs
Stages of a Drug Trial
- Preliminary Stages – initial discovery and animal testing
- Phase 1 Testing – on volunteers
- Phase 2 Testing On Patients
- Phase 3 – Large Scale Testing On Human Patients
- Phase 4 – testing after the granting of a license .

New Technology - Virtual Drug Trials & The Human Physiome Project

Among colleagues and acquaintances in the mental health sector there seems a prevalent negative attitude towards pharmaceutical companies. So I thought they deserved a fair crack of the whip in this book.

Since writing this many months ago, you will no doubt have heard about the drug trial carried out on behalf of the drug company Parexel which went disastrously wrong and lead to the hospitalisation of six healthy volunteers.

To put this into the context of the thousands of drug trials conducted annually, here is a quotation [as quoted in BBC internet news] from Richard Ley, Association of the British Pharmaceutical Industry "This is an absolutely exceptional occurrence - I cannot remember anything comparable". Human drug trials have to continue if science is to advance and we are all to benefit from life-saving new drugs. In fact, since publication of this report, many new applicants have applied for places as paid drug trail volunteers.

The Necessity of Psychiatric Drugs

I can only say that during a period of mental unwellness, I know my sanity would not have returned so quickly without antipsychotics. I had one period of psychosis without medication and would not want my worst enemy to suffer in that way. I will write about this one day when I have come to terms with the experience.

Mental health drugs, like it or not, are a necessity for some. Without drugs, they could not enjoy functional and productive lives in the community. I saw terrible suffering in the pre-drug 1950's and have researched widely enough to know this type of suffering was on a massive scale before psychiatric drugs.

There are side effects because chemical science is still in its infancy.

The Wonders of Science

Maybe one day computer mapping of the brain (covered later in this chapter) and knowledge of the human genome might bring ethically-acceptable alternatives; I mean apart from the detection and abortion of defective foetuses. However in general terms there are no cost-effective alternatives for treatment of schizophrenia, suicidal level clinical depression and psychoses.

So, whatever your view, try to read this with wonder at the skill and dedication of our scientific community. Try to think about ways in which the pharmaceuticals could become reconciled with its detractors to the benefit of both.

If there is huge profit in pharmaceuticals then one way is for more of these profits to find their way into funding mainstream services. Part of the problem is that NHS personnel are so often not trained to be business-minded. They need to become more so. Pharmaceuticals cannot afford to make losses such as the NHS sustains otherwise they would go out of business. These are the facts of business life.

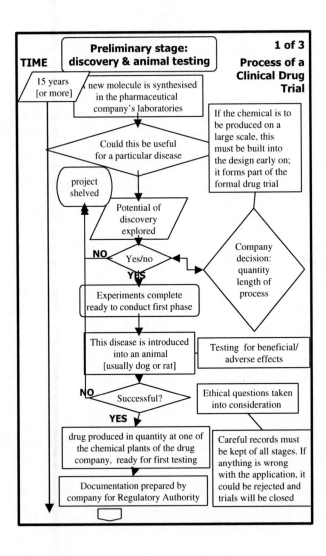

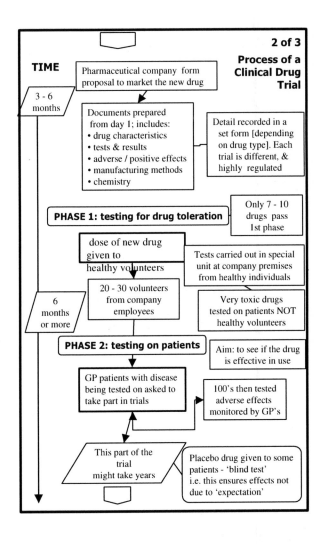

2 of 3

Process of a Clinical Drug Trial

TIME

3 - 6 months

Pharmaceutical company form proposal to market the new drug

Documents prepared from day 1; includes:
• drug characteristics
• tests & results
• adverse / positive effects
• manufacturing methods
• chemistry

Detail recorded in a set form [depending on drug type]. Each trial is different, & highly regulated

PHASE 1: testing for drug toleration

Only 7 - 10 drugs pass 1st phase

dose of new drug given to healthy volunteers

Tests carried out in special unit at company premises from healthy individuals

6 months or more

20 - 30 volunteers from company employees

Very toxic drugs tested on patients NOT healthy volunteers

PHASE 2: testing on patients

Aim: to see if the drug is effective in use

GP patients with disease being tested on asked to take part in trials

100's then tested adverse effects monitored by GP's

This part of the trial might take years

Placebo drug given to some patients - 'blind test' i.e. this ensures effects not due to 'expectation'

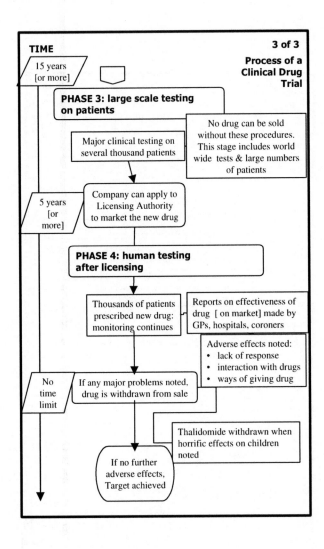

TIME

3 of 3

Process of a Clinical Drug Trial

15 years [or more]

PHASE 3: large scale testing on patients

Major clinical testing on several thousand patients

No drug can be sold without these procedures. This stage includes world wide tests & large numbers of patients

5 years [or more]

Company can apply to Licensing Authority to market the new drug

PHASE 4: human testing after licensing

Thousands of patients prescribed new drug: monitoring continues

Reports on effectiveness of drug [on market] made by GPs, hospitals, coroners

Adverse effects noted:
- lack of response
- interaction with drugs
- ways of giving drug

No time limit

If any major problems noted, drug is withdrawn from sale

Thalidomide withdrawn when horrific effects on children noted

If no further adverse effects, Target achieved

Designing and Marketing New Drugs

New drugs appear on the medical market at regular intervals. The Pharmaceutical industry and their scientists improve the quality of existing products and invent new, as they learn more about the human body. There are huge costs involved in the design and trial of new drugs and profit comes only after years of research, trials and the expenditure of millions of pounds.

An average drug takes 15 years to appear on the market. Recently there have been remarkable developments in virtual drug trials which I will describe in the last section.

Stages of a Drug Trial

Preliminary Stages – initial discovery and animal testing

Pharmaceutical companies have laboratories where chemists synthesize new drug molecules. Molecules are the small particles from which every material is made; a brick or a glass of beer.

Scientists are continually looking for new combinations of chemicals which might relieve the symptoms of an illness without too many negative effects. Negative effects are the unwanted by-products of the chemical reaction - for example some people develop stomach ache if they take aspirin. It is only when drugs are on the market that the name of these effects changes to 'side effects'.

Testing is initially carried out on laboratory animals, usually rats or dogs. The disease for which the drug is being designed is introduced into the animal and the results noted. The scientists are looking for toxicity (harmfulness) and mutagenicity (if it directly alters the structure of the organism).

Phase 1 Testing – on volunteers

After animal testing stage a trial drug is given to healthy human volunteers chosen from among pharmaceutical company employees. Public volunteers are called for at a later stage in the research. Payment for those taking part in trials is good and takes place at special centres. If you are interested in volunteering you can apply direct to the Pharmaceutical companies who will give a medical test to ensure you are suitable.

Very toxic drugs such as those designed for treating cancers are only tested on patients (i.e. people with the active disease). There are strict guidelines laid down for all human testing.

This stage of drug trial is to discover:

- how toxic the drug is - how well the body tolerates it
- how the body disposes of the drug
- comparative responses on blind trials *or placebo tests

* harmless substances are given to some volunteers and compared with responses from volunteers who have been given the test drug.

Phase 2 Testing On Patients

At phase 2, patients who have the disease are given the new drug. Tests show the effectiveness of the drugs and the dosages at which they work. When tests have been concluded and large scale trials have been carried out on patients these appear in the General Practitioners drug manual (MIMs) as side effects. All side effects have to be listed even if they occur in a few cases.

Phase 3 – Large Scale Testing On Human Patients

Human testing is an important part of the drug trial procedure and determines whether or not the new drug is allowed a licence. A large number of G.P. patients are asked for their consent to take part in the trials and are monitored for their reactions to the drug. The purpose of this part of the trial is to demonstrate the effectiveness and risk as compared with current drugs. International trials may be conducted to increase the available data. Once testing has been satisfactorily conducted (which takes up to 10 years) the Government grants a commercial license for the sale of the drug.

Phase 4 – Testing After the Granting Of A License

After the granting a license the company commences phase 4 tests which show any difficulties in long term use of the drug, such as:

- adverse reactions in long term use
- negative effects when other drugs are used at the same time (contra indications)
- revised dosage or administration methods
- looking at cases where the drug it is not effective and establishing why

Animal Testing

In some cases drug companies are able to conduct testing on tissue culture and avoid research on animals. It is questionable whether animal testing can be entirely avoided. Perhaps we had rather ask, do we want to cure virulent and painful human disease and illness and at what cost.

New Technology - Virtual Drug Trials & The Human Physiome Project

I had mentioned the Human Physiome Project in my last book and the efforts of companies such as Physiome Sciences to produce virtual (computer generated) models of the entire human body. The organisations involved world wide have now pooled resources and made the information publicly available on: http://www.physiome.org/. Do look if you are interested in seeing more about the progress of this fascinating project.

Complete virtual testing of new processes, without using animals or humans is a long way off yet and may not be in our lifetimes because of the complexity of the human body. The heart has been replicated as it is relatively straightforward but the brain contains far more complex and interdependent systems of which little is known.

Plastination

I felt I must conclude this chapter with a little about anatomist Dr Gunter Hagens. Dr Hagens invented a technique called plastination, whereby complete bodies or individual organs could be preserved indefinitely by injecting liquid plastic. This has the effect of making the organ[s] rigid yet malleable so they can be displayed in any position. Far more of the complex organs and systems of the human body can be seen by students studying his specimens than was previously possible, even computer-generated images.

Dr Hagens prepares specimens for teaching purposes but controversially turned in the late 1980's to displaying complete human corpses in artistic poses. He did this after curious visitors started flocking to see his work in Universities. Dr Hagens questioned whether his work represented science or art and decided it was a combination; showing the wonders of the human body, previously limited to those in the field of science. Judge for yourself - if you have the stomach.

'Do not wait for leaders; do it alone, person to person'
Mother Teresa

Chapter 18

Mental Health Charities

This chapter contains:
The Role of Mental Health Charities
• Changing Roles
Some Inspiring Words

After the wonders of the new virtual sciences and the controversy of Dr Hagens, let us turn our attention to those often unsung heroes who have fought long and hard to give mental health patients a voice.

The Role of Mental Health Charities

Mental Health charities are to be found world-wide offering support, advice, advocacy, legal information, treatment information and most of all pressure groups which have had far reaching effects in helping to shape the future of mental health treatment. Mental health charities have had a say in helping shape the current draft of the Mental Health Bill.

Initially, these charities fought issues on behalf of hospitalised patients too ill or demented to represent themselves. With better medication, more effective treatments and increasing self confidence, mental health service users are finding their own voices.

Changing Roles

Perhaps the role of mental health charities will be different by the time I revise this book. However, they do have a vital educative role to play, reducing stigma and fighting for full social inclusion, the dream of everyone who cares about the field.

Rather than a stack of facts I think it is time I leave you to start your own exploration. I have listed some of the larger organisations in the 'further information' section towards the end of this book. For those of you who are not yet computer literate (shame on you!) try your local libraries which are bursting with helpful Library staff and information at your fingertips.

Some Inspiring Words

I thought you might like to read some inspiring quotations which I have chosen from the mission statements of the larger organisations. These encapsulate what is best about the world wide move towards improving life for those with mental illness and to ensure mental health for all.

If you have read this book so far I hope by now you are enthused to go off and search for more information on your pet subject. Remember, reduction of stigma is not the work of mental health charities, clinicians, patients nor carers alone. You as an individual can contribute something, however small you consider that to be.

Think about what you can do and be inspired by some of the following heartfelt words. And remember, 1 in 4 - it could be you.

Mind

"Our vision is of a society that promotes and protects good mental health for all, and that treats people with experience of mental distress fairly, positively, and with respect."

****

Sane

"Information is not a cure for mental illness but we believe that knowledge can bring relief."

Rethink (formerly NSF)

"..by working together we can create a culture of hope, support and recovery that embodies a belief in people's own ability to manage, change and improve the quality of their lives."

****

Together (formerly MACA)

"We are about people working together for happiness."

****

YoungMinds (babies, children & young people)

"Our mission is all about working 'beyond the professional' to ensure that children's mental health is truly the business of everybody."

****

Mental Health Organisation (latest campaign of)

"Together with Sustain: the alliance for better farming and food, we have launched a campaign to increase awareness and understanding of the links between food and mental health."

****

Sign (National Society for Mental Health and Deafness)

"We aim for a world where there is little risk of deaf people developing preventable mental health problems and that equality, respect and fulfilment are enjoyed by [them]."

****

MDF (bipolar affective disorder)

"Between mood swings people with ... Bipolar Affective Disorder feel and behave like anyone else with the ordinary ups and downs that anyone can experience."

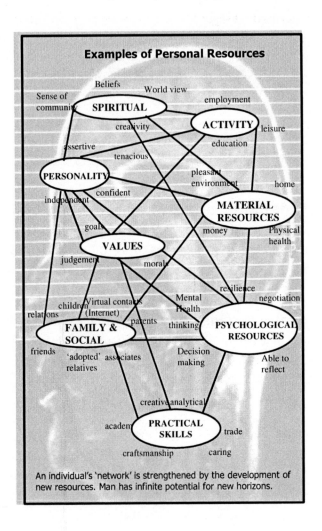

Examples of Personal Resources

Beliefs
World view
Sense of community
employment
SPIRITUAL
creativity
ACTIVITY
leisure
assertive
education
tenacious
PERSONALITY
pleasant environment
home
confident
independent
MATERIAL RESOURCES
goals
money
Physical health
VALUES
judgement
moral
resilience
negotiation
children
Virtual contacts (Internet)
Mental Health
relations
parents
thinking
PSYCHOLOGICAL RESOURCES
FAMILY & SOCIAL
friends
'adopted' relatives
associates
Decision making
Able to reflect
creative
analytical
academ
PRACTICAL SKILLS
trade
craftsmanship
caring

An individual's 'network' is strengthened by the development of new resources. Man has infinite potential for new horizons.

236

"Perhaps the ability to distance oneself from over-involvement with others ..the capacity to make a coherent pattern of one's life, are .. important factors in .. peace of mind and maintaining mental health".
Anthony Storr, Solitude

Chapter 19

Help Yourself to Mental Health

This Chapter contains:
What Is A Meaningful Life?
A Sense of Friendship and Belonging
Sense of Making/ Creating
Sense of Spirituality
Being Alone

Well we are nearing the end of a long marathon together. By now I hope you will have a good idea of what understanding mental illness really means, from a wide variety of views.

Perhaps you have thought about your own mental health or that of someone in your family, your circle of friends, colleagues or hobbyists. Mental health for all is the vision of everyone in the field and it means the community working together for the common good. It also means an individual view.

What does mental health mean to you; how can you retain it in this stressed out, heavily sensation-flooded and information saturated world? No one has all the answers and indeed this is a journey we have to work out for ourselves as those wise people at the website Mental Health Matters say.

I have gathered together a few ideas but this is your chapter. Take some time out to write down or draw or paint or sing your personal mental health plan. Good luck! I hope you have enjoyed sharing this journey with me and I'll maybe catch up with you later on your journey through the pages of another book.

Maintaining Psychological Balance
The Importance of Psychological Support

Psychological health
This person has strong
psychological supports
which help resist life pressures

stress

bereavement

COMMUNITY LINKS

LOVE

SECURITY

FRIENDS

ageing

abuse

FAMILY

BELIEFS

HEALTH

illness

Poor psychological health

With no support systems life pressures are more likely to affect
balance of mind. In my examples external pressure is identical.

stress

bereavement

SOCIAL ISOLATION

NSECURITY

LONELINE

ageing

abuse

ISOLATION

LACK OF
SELF WORTH

illness

What Is A Meaningful Life?

When you are young and fit, a meaningful life might consist of enough money to entertain and clothe yourself. As mature adults we come to see things in a different light but nevertheless money looms large in many requirement lists. So, apart from winning the lottery or getting that ab fab job what are the requirements for a meaningful life?

A Sense of Friendship and Belonging

Human beings are social on the whole. Belonging could mean a social group, sharing ideals, or sharing a common interest with others. If you prefer your own company, there are still plenty of opportunities to share virtual space in the many web communities, knowledge cafes, chat rooms, newsgroups and gaming societies.

You can be alone in a room full of people or feel socially welcome having a chat or sharing emails alone in your room.

Never let anyone say that X is right and Y is wrong. 21st century life has provided more benefits through advanced technology than our 19th century forbears could have dreamed of...

Sense of Making/ Creating

Creating or performing are satisfying, keep the brain alert and exercise the body. Concentrating on a form, an action or a piece of writing takes the mind into another dimension, the pleasure areas of the brain. Absorption in this type of activity enables the mind to bypass negative emotions and make sense of the situation. It is therapeutic and enjoyable at the same time.

Anyone can write creatively. Years ago, I edited and published an anthology of poetry written by in-patients. Those who had their poetry published were thrilled their work had been appreciated by a wider public. You don't have to be Shakespeare or Wordsworth to create something worthwhile and enjoyable and you don't have to be a professional; there are many opportunities out there if you care to look. If you have had emotional problems that will actually help because you will have a depth of feeling to call upon that is unique.

Sense of Spirituality

Many people confuse the terms religious and spiritual. Spirituality is in the makeup of everyone providing it is developed. Once the mind has been opened up to individual spirituality it can bring enormous comfort and a vibrant sense of psychological belonging. Those recovered from depressive illness, which have experienced a spiritual awareness opening, will realize that hope often hides within the darkness. Hope is another dimension of spirituality.

Being Alone

The quotation at the head of this chapter is a wonderful example of how being alone is positively beneficial from the point of view of your mental health. That was the original intention for Asylums, as places of refuge. Maybe the Victorians were along the right lines in one sense.

The isolation of depression and other mental illness is very hard to bear. However, I think this eventually teaches that isolation is not a physical fact but a state of mind.

You may have experienced the deep loneliness of being in a crowded party, yet felt a warm sense of belonging as you walked alone in a favourite spot, surrounded by the sublime feelings, sounds, sights, and smells of nature. That is the difference between being alone and loneliness.

Being alone is the only time we have to come to terms with the past, think about our experiences, make sense of our lives.

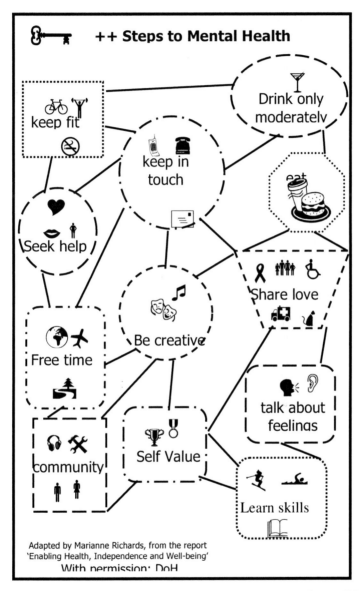

++ Steps to Mental Health

keep fit

Drink only moderately

keep in touch

eat

Seek help

Share love

Be creative

Free time

talk about feelings

community

Self Value

Learn skills

Adapted by Marianne Richards, from the report
'Enabling Health, Independence and Well-being'
With permission: DoH

Hermits down the centuries have chosen their solitary life to contemplate their God in the silences of their own hearts. Many creatives, and I count myself as one, enjoy being alone for long periods at a time. It is the greatest gift of love you can give yourself.

The Pleasures of Life

Life's greatest pleasures, after tragedy, are often simple. These are a few of mine:

- ♥ peace of mind - (freedom from depression, voices & hallucinations)
- ♥ the silence before storms, the thunder and rain and the sense of calmness
- ♥ the first snowdrops of spring
- ♥ sitting down with a glass of wine after hard work
- ♥ the sounds of nature and of evocative music
- ♥ the privilege of sharing my journey, my experiences and my learning with you

"Give knowledge to a wise man, and he will be yet wiser"
Anon

Chapter 20

Further Sources of Information

This Chapter contains:

Art & Movies about Life
Book lists by subject
Interesting Web sites by subject

I have included my research reading in this chapter because this book is not an academic textbook. I apologise in advance to authors I've omitted in error and will make necessary corrections in future editions if informed.

Medical, psychological and analytical books explain why things happen but the creative arts bring fact to life. Movies can show the experience of mental illness more graphically than any textbook. My reading list contains poetry, fiction and web sites as well as easy-to-understand medical books.

If you don't like meeting people or are too shy to ask librarians for books you want trying searching on the Internet. Virtual information arrives instantly. There are many sites, particularly in the USA, which give have very useful information. Americans are less inhibited about mental health.

A word of caution; start with sites which give sound information such as university websites (denoted by '.ac' for academic); major mental health charities; government websites (denoted by '.gov').

The following are in alphabetical order by subject.

ART & MOVIES ABOUT LIFE

Any paintings   **William Blake**
An artist who successfully portrays madness and suffering

The Plains of Heaven   **John Martin**
One of a trilogy about The Day of Judgement

One Flew Over the Cuckoos Nest   **movie**
Now made into an award-winning movie, the book is a fictional account about lobotomy

Shine   **movie**
Based on the true story of concert pianist David Helfgott who had a nervous breakdown but later married and came back to the concert hall

A Beautiful Mind   **movie**
Based on the true story of mathematician Dr John Nash, diagnosed with schizophrenia, he later became a Nobel prize winner

The Rain Man   **movie**
Based on the true story of autistic savant Kim Peek

Any drawings   **Stephen Wiltshire**
Stephen Wiltshire was born autistic yet makes his living as an aclaimed architectural artist

BOOKS ABOUT LIFE

Anthony Storr   **Solitude**
An readable book about the art of living alone.

Viktor Frankl   **Man's Search for Meaning**
Dr Frankl's own logotherapy, explained within the context of his own experiences during the holocaust.

Scott Peck   **The Road Less Travelled**

Scott Peck's own journey of self-discovery.

Khalil Gibran   **The Prophet**

A book about life by a poet and philosopher.

Benjamin Hoff   **The Tao of Pooh**

Re-discovering the child inside you. Based on the Pooh Bear books by A A Milne

Benjamin Hoff   **The Te of Piglet**

Another book based on Pooh, this time about the shy piglet and what he has to offer life.

Richard Bach   **Jonathan Livingston Seagull**

An modern myth about a seagull who dares to be different.

A. De Saint-Exupéry   **The Little Prince**

An allegory about life in the form of the story of a young prince's travels.

H G Wells   **The Door in the Wall**

A book about perceptions. Is the door a gateway to paradise or a false dream?

Thich Nhat Hanh   **The miracle of mindfulness**

All about mindfulness, a type of meditation now increasingly common in the NHS.

BIOGRAPHIES/DIARIES

Kay Redfield Jamison   **An Unquiet Mind**

Dr Jamison's own experience of manic-depressive illness

Jacki Lyden   **Daughter of the Queen of Sheba**

Jacki's mother was diagnosed with mania and almost destroyed the lives of her family

Anne Frank   **The Diary of Anne Frank**

The tragic diary of a young girl who dreamed of being an author and wrote her story during the three years her Jewish family hid from the Nazis, before being betrayed.

Viktor Frankl   **Viktor Frankl Recollections**

A very moving autobiography. Frankl survived Auschwitz but years later committed suicide.

THERAPY AND PERSONAL DEVELOPMENT

Edited by Sidney Rosen   **My voice Will Go With You: Teaching Tales of Milton Erickson**

Teaching metaphors of the late American psychiatrist Milton Erickson, pioneer of the solution focused (brief) therapy methods.

Irvin Yalom Psychotherapist   **Love's Executioner and Other Tales of Psychotherapy**

Interesting cases from the couch of Irvin Yalom.

Lauren Slater   **Welcome to My Country**

More tales of psychotherapeutic encounters with mental illness.

Dr Margaret Reinhold   **How to Survive In Spite of Your Parents**

A practical self-help book and an explanation of Dr Reinhold's theory and work.

Shakti Gawain **Creative Visualisation**

A favourite with 'New Age' people, and a useful introduction to the art of visualisation as a life enhancing technique.

José Silva **The Silva Mind Technique**

Exercises to improve memory, concentration, and break free of self-limiting patterns of thinking.

Eric Berne **Games People Play**

Dr Berne sees through those irritating life games people play, and teaches you how to recognise and avoid them.

Swami Paramananda **Self Mastery**

A little book by an acknowledged master of Eastern spiritual traditions.

Joseph Goldstein **Insight Meditation: The Practice of Freedom**

Buddhist Vipassana meditation.

Dr David D Burns **Feeling Good, The New Mood Therapy**

Based on cognitive therapy, this is a practical book on self-help techniques for depressive illness.

RESEARCH & HISTORY OF MENTAL ILLNESS

Roy Porter **A Brief History of Madness**

An easy-to-read history of mental illness and its treatment.

American Psychiatric Association **DSM IV**

The diagnostic manual used by psychiatrists world wide to diagnose mental illness. See also websites

J Andrews, J Briggs et al   The History of Bethlem

A history of the earliest of the Asylums.

Sainsbury Centre for   Beyond the Water
Mental Health   Towers

Up to date expert papers on aspects of the treatment of mental
illness, from asylums to the present day. Very readable.

A Rogers   Behavioural Sciences &
the Law

A paper around treatment with ECT

CASE STUDIES

Malcolm Macmillan   An Odd Kind of Fame:
Stories of Phineas Gage

The author is a well-known psychiatrist, This book is about the
Victorian man who's accident inspired research into the functional
areas of the brain, and also the infamous lobotomy.

Oliver Sacks   The Man Who Thought
His Wife Was a Hat

The author is a well-known psychiatrist who writes interesting
vignettes about aphasia, an illness which prevents patients
properly translating what they see.

Virginia Axline   Dibs, in Search of Self

How a lost child was brought back into the world by a
Psychotherapist.

Dr Kay Redfield Jamison   Touched with Fire

A book covering the them of manic depression and creativity.

MISCELLANEOUS

Peter Tatham   The Makings of
Maleness

A Jungian Analyst writes about modern man and uses the Greek
myth of Daedalus to illustrate the modern archetypal male figure.

Interesting Websites

Copy and paste these web addresses (URL's) below into the address window at the top of your web browser page. They were current at the time of publication of this book.

BOOKSHOPS ON-LINE

http://bookmag.com/books/nonfiction/168.html
Mental Health books

http://www.mind.org.uk/osb/showitem.cfm/Category/0
MIND's own bookshop

CARERS ORGANISATIONS

http://www.carersuk.org/Home
Information and advice for carers

http://www.youngminds.org.uk
A site for young carers

COMPLEMENTARY MEDICINE WEBSITES

http://www.baat.org/
British Art Therapy Association

http://www.acupuncture.org.uk
British Acupuncture Council

http://www.bcp.org.uk/
British Psychoanalytic Council

http://www.bsmt.org/
British Society for Music Therapy

http://www.bwy.org.uk/
British Wheel of Yoga

http://www.mctimoney-college.ac.uk/contact.htm
McTimoney Chiropractic

http://www.homeopathy-soh.org/
Society of Homeopaths

http://www.rchm.co.uk/
The Register of Chinese Herbal Medicine

GENERAL INFORMATION ABOUT MENTAL HEALTH

http://www.patient.org.uk/
Patient UK. All aspects of medicine

http://www.amazon.com/exec/obidos/tg/detail/-
/0890420254/104-9193091-6903963?v=glance
Link to DSM IV (diagnostic manual) on Amazon

http://www.mentalhealth.org.uk/html/content/voices.cfm
Useful information for those who hear voices from a mental
health organisation

http://www.samaritans.org.uk/
Samaritans (offer an email counselling service)

http://www.edauk.com/
Eating Disorders Association (UK)

http://www.selfharmalliance.org/
Self Harm Alliance

http://www.mdf.org.uk/

MDF The Bi Polar Organisation

HISTORICAL ASPECTS OF MENTAL HEALTH

http://www.mdx.ac.uk/www/study/mhhglo.htm#Asylums

http://www.channel4.com/science/microsites/S/science/body/timeline.html

Timeline from Channel 4 of the history of mental illness

http://www.hypnoanalysis.com/history-of-hypnosis.html#

International Association of Hypno Analysts - a history of hypnosis

http://medhist.ac.uk/index.html

Wellcome Trust's website - history of mental illness

LEGAL ASPECTS OF MENTAL HEALTH

http://www.hyperguide.co.uk/mha/

A guide to the Mental Health Act - private user site

http://www.nice.org.uk/pdf/ECT_Final_panel_response.pdf

Acrobat (pdf) version of the NICE 2003 report on ECT panel decision against appeal

http://news.bbc.co.uk/1/hi/talking_point/2676039.stm

BBC talking point – public views on the question "is suicide justified?"

http://www.alzheimers.org.uk/pdf/i_LivingWill.pdf

Acrobat (pdf) file of the Alzheimers Society explaining living wills

MEDICATION

http://www.rcpsych.ac.uk/info/factsheets/pfacanti.asp

Royal College of Psychiatrists factsheet on antidepressants

MENTAL HEALTH ORGANISATIONS

http://www.who.int/mental_health/evidence/en/atlas_chapt _1_2_eng.pdf

The World Mental Health Atlas project [mapping global mental health services]

http://www.depressionalliance.org/

Mental health generally

http://www.samaritans.org.uk/know/statistics.shtm

Samaritans on-line

http://www5.who.int/mental_health/main.cfm?p=00000001 49

World Health Organisation – mental health section

http://www.sane.org.uk/public_html/index.shtml

SANE & saneline (helpline) mental health charity website

http://www.together-uk.org/index.asp?id=1

Together mental health charity (formerly MACA)

http://www.rethink.org/

Rethink (formerly National Schizophrenia Fellowship) mental health charity

http://www.depressionalliance.org/

The Depression Alliance mental health charity

http://www.retreat-hospital.org/

The Retreat hospital. Care for anyone with mental health problems (York Retreat)

www.turning-point.co.uk
Turning Point, for mental health rehabilitation & counselling

www.mind.org.uk
MIND, the mental health charity

http://www.depressionalliance.org/
Depression alliance mental health charity

http://www.rcpsych.ac.uk/
Royal College of Psychiatrists information on all aspects of mental illness

http://www.londonhealth.co.uk/carersnationalassociation.asp
Carers National Association

PSYCHOANALYSIS

http://www.freud.org.uk/Index.html
The Freud Museum

http://www.jungiananalysts.org.uk/
Jungian Analysts Organisation

SCIENCE & TECHNOLOGY

http://www.parkinsonalliance.org/
Parkinson Alliance

http://www.parkinsonsappeal.com/news.html
News about the deep brain stimulation method

THERAPIES

http://www.cognitivetherapy.com/
Cognitive Behavioural Therapy
http://www.priory.com/dbt.htm
Dialectical Behavioural Therapy

http://www.butler-bowdon.com/manssearch.htm
http://www.hypnos.co.uk/hypnomag/pdurbin4.htm
About Victor Frankl and human trinity therapy

http://www.petsastherapy.org/Visiting/VisitingScheme.htm
Pets as Therapy

http://www.greengym.org.uk/
Green Gym

TRAINING

http://www.rgu.ac.uk/subj/pharmacy/pharmacy.htm
School of Pharmacy web site

http://www.hull.ac.uk/home/prospectus/undergrad/social_
work.html
Training in Social Work

http://www.npa.co.uk/
National Pharmacists Association

http://www.acpp.org.uk
Association for Child Psychology & Psychiatry

http://www.uncommon-
knowledge.co.uk/milton_erickson/family_therapy.html
http://www.creativity.co.uk/creativity/guhen/erickson.htm
About the founder of all brief therapies - Dr Milton Erickson

http://www.newtherapist.com/20hitch.html
an amusing journey through brief therapy, in metaphorical style

http://www.n-shap-ericksonian.co.uk/Erickson.htm
Ericksonian brief therapy and NLP

http://www.brieftherapy.org.uk/
Brief Therapy Organisation - training

Glossary

A

acupuncture — Chinese system of healing using needles to balance energies

acute stage — period when an illness worsens

activity therapy — treatment based on work, education or play

acupuncture — Chinese medical treatment for re-balancing the body's energies

Advocate — someone who supports or pleads on another's behalf

affective disorders — problems with mood

affirmations — one line sayings, used for the same purpose as visualisations

agitation — see psychomotor

agoraphobia — fear of open spaces

akathisia — restlessness, unable to sit or stand

alleviate — relieve the symptoms of

alternative medicine — alternatives to conventional drug therapies & medical treatments

anaesthetic — drugs which render a patient unconscious or impervious to pain

analgesic — pain killing drug

Analysand — a person who attends for psycho analysis

Analytical Psychology — a psychological therapy devised by Carl Jung

anatomy — the study of the human body

ancestor worship — culture of venerating dead ancestors

anorexia nervosa — eating disorder in which a person restricts their intake of food

antidepressant — drug which reduces the symptoms of depressive illness

antimanic — drug which reduces the symptoms of a manic episode

antipsychotic — drug - reduces psychosis

anti social — a personality disorder, characterised by difficulties in socialising

256

anxiety	state of arousal in which a person experiences unpleasant feelings
aphasia	sensory loss resulting in inability to understand the surroundings
Apothecary	historic term for Pharmacist [also: Druggist, Chemist, Chymist]
Approved Social Worker	ASW; Social Worker who detains under the Mental Health Act
arachnophobia	fear of spiders
archetype	a specific character trait within the personality (Jungian theory)
aromatherapy	a body massage with aromatic oils
art therapy	a therapy for emotional problems using art, music or drama
assertive	someone psychologically confident and outgoing
Asylum	Victorian institute for insane people. Literally 'a place of refuge'.
'at risk' [people]	[in mental health] people likely to become mentally ill
audio [hallucinations]	imagined voices which no one else can hear
autonomous system	automatic bodily functioning [heart beat, breathing]
avoidant	personality disorder, characterised by avoiding situations

B

BAC	British Association for Counselling (Umbrella organisation)
'bad trip'	bad experience on illegal drugs
balanced personality	someone who has developed their mental and spiritual capacities
'basic means'	a minimal amount of money or resources to live on; no frills
behaviour	the things which we do; the way in which we react to situations
behaviour pattern	reacting in a consistent way to certain types of people/situation

behavioural therapy	a psychological therapy aimed at modifying behaviour (actions)
Bethlem Asylum	second oldest Hospital in England; a former Victorian Asylum
Bible/ 'bible'	Christian holy book; 'bible' - used to mean a useful guide to life
bi-polar	a mental illness; alternating episodes of depression and mania
bile (black bile)	one of the 4 'humours'; responsible for depression (see 'humour')
binge eating	uncontrolled eating of vast amounts of food before purging it
'blind trials'	inert drugs given to prove that the real drugs are having an effect
blood/infection phobia	fear of blood, or of being infected by dirt, needles etc
blood letting	releasing blood - historic treatment for mental illness
BMA	British Medical Association; professional body for medicine
borderline	a mild personality disorder
BPS	British Psychological Society for training UK Psychologists
brain chemistry	the chemicals of the brain, produced by chemical transmitters
brain fever	historic term describing what is probably psychosis
brain pacemaker	device which prevents tremors [see deep brain stimulation]
brain scan	scans show electrical activity or physical damage in the brain
brief psychotic disorder	mental illness of brief duration, brought on by stress reaction
Breuer Joseph	famous Victorian practitioner of hypnosis; forerunner of Freud
Britishness	the tendency of British people 'not to interfere' or share feelings
Broadmoor	a psychiatric hospital for the criminally insane

Buddhism	spiritual order which follows the teaching of Gautama Buddha
bulimia	eating disorder, characterised by bouts of purging and vomiting

C

Community Care Act	Legislation for closure of Asylums
care plan	a written document, outlining proposed care for a client/ patient
carer	someone who cares for another person, usually voluntarily
case history	details of patient's life, with a psychological and physical history
case notes	records kept by therapists of client sessions, usually brief notes
catatonia	mental state characterised by total lack of movement and energy
catharsis	Greek for purging; in psychology the 'letting go' of a negative trait
CDPOM	drug which can only be dispensed on a handwritten prescription
Charcot Jean Martin	famous Victorian Doctor and hypnotist; forerunner of Freud
'checking and testing'	trait of compulsive disorder; excessive checking
chemical imbalance	imbalance of mood-enhancing chemicals - serotonin or dopamine
chemical transmitter	the way brain chemicals are distributed to all of the brain cells
Chemist	scientist who has trained in preparing drugs and medications
chen	in Chinese medicine the life force
chi	the body's mental alertness or happiness in Chinese medicine
Chinese herbal medicine	Treatment using herbs as medicines
Chiropractic	manipulation of the spine and joints; re-aligns skeletal system

Chymist	historic term - Pharmacist [see Apothecary, Chemist, Druggist,]
Cinderella	Archetypal fictional character, representing innocence rewarded
claustrophobia	fear of confined spaces
Clinical Psychologist	psychologist who practices within medical setting
clinical responsibility	legal responsibility for patient's well-being
clinical trial	testing of new drugs
clinician	a person who practices medicine [clinic - Greek word for 'bed']
CMHT	Community Mental Health Team; mental health professionals
cognitive-behavioural	therapy for recognition and change of poor behaviour patterns
cohort	group with common characteristics e.g. trainees on a course
comatose	in a coma-like state, unable to respond to people
complementary	non medical treatments e.g. herbal, acupuncture, art therapy
complementary therapies	therapies not based on medical teaching; additional to medicine
compliance (of patient)	extent to which patients will willingly take prescribed drugs
compulsion	an urge to carry out a certain act or ritual
computer modelling	making accurate models of the body and brain using computers
conditioned response	theory that human behaviour depends upon an outside stimulus
conflict (mental)	two or more opposing events, motives, behaviours, impulses
conscious (mind)	part of the mind aware of its actions
'container' [in therapy]	a means or process of conducting therapy (virtual)
contra indicative	reacts badly with other chemicals (applied to certain drugs)

conversion disorder	a neurotic problem becoming a physical disorder e.g. paralysis
convulsion	involuntary shaking, such as in epilepsy or Parkinson's Disease
copycat suicides	methods of suicide which are copied from published reports
copyright	a law which forbids the copying of someone else's creative work
counselling	one of the talking cures
Counsellor	mental health professional who offers a talking cure
crime of passion	a crime which was committed during an intense emotion (France)
cross-disciplinary	anything which includes more than one profession
curse	an act of wishing death, illness or other evil upon another person
Cruse	an organisation which provides bereavement counselling

D

DBS	deep brain stimulation (see below)
de-sensitising	therapeutic way of gradually exposing someone to their fear
dead-end job	work with no prospect of further training or learning
deep brain stimulation	method of relieving tremors by stimulating specific brain cells
Delphic Oracle	famous prophetess of Ancient Greece
delusion	ideas which are perceived as real, but are only in the imagination
dementia	usually irreversible brain damage with reduction in intellect
demon	another term for a devil or evil spirit
dependent	personality disorder characterised by clinging to another person
depot injection	monthly injection, usually in the buttocks or thigh
'depressive'	derogatory term for someone with depressive illness

261

depressive illness	mental illness, characterised by intense hopelessness and sadness
Dervish	Islamic sect of holy men who perform a whirling dance - sema
developmental stage	the age at which certain specific skills are generally learned
diagnosis	deducing illness from observation, or facts given by the patient
Diagnostic & Statistics IV	manual for diagnosing mental illness as used by psychiatrists
disembodied voices	voices heard when no one is around.
DNA	chemicals which carry the characteristics of human life
dna	a term meaning 'did not attend'
DNR	'do not resuscitate'; doctor's directive
dopamine	chemical affecting motor activity e.g. tremors, or lack of activity
'double edged sword'	has both bad and good points
'downsizing'	euphemism for making many workers redundant
drama therapy	patient/therapist 'act out' scenes from their life, with new endings
Druggist	historic term - Pharmacist [see Apothecary, Chemist & Chymist]
drugs	medications; also used as a colloquial term for illegal drugs
drugs round (the)	in hospitals medications are dispensed during the drugs round
DSM (IV)	see ' Diagnostic & Statistics Manual'
DSPD	dangerous severely personality disordered e.g. psychopath
dual diagnosis	someone with two diagnosed conditions e.g. mental and physical
dynamics [e.g. of a group]	way relationships change and develop
dystonia	abnormal face and body movements, e.g. pacing, tapping the feet

E

eating disorders	illness characterised by restricting food intake by various means
eccentric	someone/ something that does not conform to accepted standards
Electro Convulsive Therapy	(ECT) electric shock treatment given to treat chronic depression or the symptoms of schizophrenia; restricted in use by NICE.
EEG	electro-encephalograph (brain scan machine)
electric eels	historic treatment for madness; crude form of ECT
electro-encephalograph	reading on a printed tape or monitor of electrical brain activity
empathy	having an understanding of a personal situation
epilepsy	interruption of electric flow to the brain causing fits
episodic [mental illness]	periods of mental illness followed by periods of normality
ethical	responsibility to abide by the moral code in a particular situation
euthanasia	'mercy killing'; ending the life of terminally ill
evidence-based medicine	medicine which is proven through research to be effective
evil spirits	imaginary entities who were blamed for episodes of madness
expressed emotion	feelings that are expressed e.g. by crying, laughing, shouting
externalised	inward emotion/experience, experienced as if an outside event
extrovert	outgoing, confident personality

F

fantasy	events imagined as if they were real
forensic psychiatry	psychiatric work with criminal mental illness e.g. psychopathic

formulate	term used for the making of medications/ pills by doctors
fractal	a fragment, like the fragments forming the patterns of a crystal
'fragmenting'	the experience of psychosis, or losing touch with the real world
Frankl Viktor	Jewish psychiatrist; author of 'Man's Search for Meaning'.
free association	method devised by Freud for finding meaningful connections between specific words used by his patients
Freud Sigmund	Founder of psycho analysis
fringe [medicine]	medicine not generally accepted by the medical profession
frontal lobes	frontal area of the brain responsible for personality and mood

G

General Practitioner	a medical doctor who practices in a general medical setting
genetic factor	attributed to inherited genes i.e. beyond control of patient
genome	collection of human genes; genes determine the personality
geriatric	medicine of old age
Gesundheit Institute	Dr Patch Adams USA clinic for humour and creative therapies
'giro'	slang for benefit cheque given in the form of a giro cheque
giving an illness a name	diagnosing; giving an illness a name prior to treating it
grandiose ideas	delusional belief e.g. a patient believes he is God or a prophet
Green Paper	proposals for changes to legislation, inviting comment
Group Home	homes for several ex- patients living together
group therapy	a therapy conducted with one therapist and several patients

GSL	general sale list; drugs available for sale at a Pharmacy

H

hallucination - sound	unreal voices or sounds
hallucination - visual	seeing things which are not real
Haloperidol	medication which prevents the symptoms of mania
'handle' [on the Internet]	term for a nickname used when not wishing to give a real name
'hard' drugs	highly addictive drugs such as cocaine, heroin and morphine
Herbalist	therapist who prescribes herbs
hero	Jungian archetype - hero myth of birth, death & resurrection
'high'	exaggerated emotion
Hippocrates	Greek Philosopher who made a study of the human mind
histrionic	personality disorder - exaggerated emotions
holistic therapy	mind body and spirit
homeopathy	diluted herbs which mimic & heal the symptoms experienced
homicidal	an urgency to commit murder
hostile environment	living in difficult conditions, e.g. housing, financial, social
'hot bed'	slang; places where people with particular characteristics gather
hovel	historic term for poor quality or 'slum' housing
humour or 'vital fluid'	in ancient medicine, 4 life-giving fluids in the body
Hypno-Psychotherapist	therapist who practices brief therapy with hypnosis
hypnosis	bypassing conscious mind by inducing relaxation
hypnotic state	state of relaxation [see trance]
hysteria	historic term - loss of control

hysterical paralysis	paralysis due mental problem [see conversion disorder]

I

identity	the things around and within us which make us individual
imbalance [brain]	brain's chemicals are not properly distributed; leading to illness
impulse	a powerful desire to do or act out
innate	inborn
individuation	Jungian concept of the process of becoming a unique person
inhibitor	chemical which prevents a normal reaction from taking place
insanity	state of mind where the mental processes are not functioning
insight	ability to understand the psychological situation
institutionalisation	deterioration of independence caused by long periods in hospital
Internet	a linked web of computers which can exchange information
intractable	mental illness which is ingrained and difficult to treat
introspective	'looking inward'; a way of thinking about what has happened
introvert	thinking, inward looking personality
isolation	feeling different or separate from other people

J

jing	Chinese medicine; a person's ability for growth (cf genes)
Jung CG	founder of Analytical Psychology & modern psychotherapies
Jungian Analyst	follower of the Jungian school

K

kaleidoscope	telescope-like toy; crystals form patterns by turning an outer tube
Koran	holy book of the Islamic religion

L

Laing R. D.	psychiatrist who believed mental illness was a social condition
'land her one'	slang for physical violence
lay person	someone not formally trained in a particular discipline
legislation	laws passed by Government and approved by the Queen
leucotomy (lobotomy)	psychosurgery, cutting the frontal lobes of the brain
learning disability	condition where the intellect is damaged due to brain damage
lesioning	method of surgically destroying individual damaged brain cells
librium	tranquilliser prescribed to many women - see also 'valium'
'life event'	an event which is vivid enough to be remembered long afterward
lifekeeper jewellery	jewellery depicting symbols of the preciousness of human life
'liquid cosh'	slang term for lithium or medications which dampen mood
lithium	naturally occurring metallic salts used in the treatment of mania
lobotomy	see leucotomy
locum	a temporary doctor, replacing a doctor who is away for any reason
loop holes (lacuna)	areas of law which are not clearly set out
Lord Chancellor	Senior Judge in English Law
lunatic	historic term for madness (belief that the moon caused madness)

M

MACA	see 'Together'
'mad'	derogatory; someone who acts in a strange way
Madhouse	historic term - Asylum
madness	derogatory slang term describing people with mental illness

mannerism	particular trait, such as a tic, grimace or other involuntary action
mania	mental illness, characterised by intense moods/ frantic behaviour
maniac	historic term - person with mania
manic	extreme excitement
manic episode	a period of mania
MAOI's	monoamine oxidase inhibitors; antidepressants
mapping	collecting and collating information, and publishing the results
mastery and pleasure	a programme of self help for clients with depressive illness
MBBS	the doctorate or degree conferred on General Practitioners
'media image'	'type' of person idealised in the media
medical model	the theory of those who practice medicine i.e. use of medications
medication	drugs given to cure or alleviate the symptoms of an illness
melancholia	an early term for depressive illness
memory quilts	quilts embossed with pictures of deceased, to demonstrate the human tragedy of suicide (instead of publishing bland statistics)
MENSA	social group for people with high intellect
mental defective	historic term - see 'social misfit'
mental handicap	permanently damaged brain (cerebral palsy); term no longer used
Mental Health Act 1983	Government guidelines for the treatment of mental illness
Mental Health Bill 2004	new legislation for mental health, about to become law (2006)
Mental Health Tribunal	group empowered to detain/ release psychiatric hospital patients
Mental Health Team	group of mental health workers from different professions
Mental Health Worker	similar to 'Rehabilitation Officer'

mental illness	illness of the mind, not 'physical illness; treatable not curable
Mental Nurse	therapist qualified to administer psychiatric drugs
mid life crisis	anxiety about achievements & the future said to occur at mid life
Milton Erickson	American psychiatrist who invented brief therapy
MIMS	manual of drugs and their characteristics, used by GPs
Mind	national mental health charity
mindfulness	the practice of a state of complete awareness in all tasks
misnomer	term 'the name does not describe the thing itself adequately'
model	a pattern or opinion used as an example; or a computer simulation
modelling (of humans)	programmes which replicate the functions of the human body
molecule	smallest particle of matter
mood	changing experiences of feelings e.g. happiness, sadness, anger
mood swings (rapid)	rapid mood changes
moral maze	complex moral questions
moral therapy	reward & punishment used to change unwanted behaviours
motor neurone disease	terminal illness which systematically destroys the nervous system
muscle relaxant	drug given to relax the muscles before surgery to prevent injury
music therapy	type of art therapy using music to induce and counter mood
mutagenicity	ability of a drug to affect the chemistry of organs in the body

N

narcissistic	personality disorder characterised by extreme self interest

'negative effect'	at drug trial stage, unwanted reactions (after marketing the drugs, these will be published under the term 'side effects')
nervous breakdown	slang term for a mental illness; brief psychotic disorder
neuro transmitters (brain)	nerve cells containing chemical messengers affecting mood
NICE	Natl. Inst. of Clinical Excellence - clinical evidence research org.
NLP	'neuro-linguistic programming'; brief therapy method
noradrenaline	chemical transmitter in the brain (see also serotonin)
normalizing	making a condition acceptable; can be positive or negative

O

obsession	unhealthy preoccupation with something or someone
obsessive-compulsive	mental illness, characterised by obsessions and compulsions
OCD	Obsessional-Compulsive Disorder
Oedipus complex	theory that children fall in love with the parent of opposite sex
'old lag'	one who commits petty crimes, in order to remain in prison
on-the-job training	training by working; common in medical and social work fields
open up	express emotions freely
Orwell, George	Victorian social author who wrote about working lives
Osteopathy	therapy involving manipulation of spine (see also chiropractic)
ostracised	excluded from a group because of beliefs or other petty reasons
'over-prescribing'	bad prescribing to calm mood e.g. anger in crotchety old patients

P

P [medication packs]	Pharmacist must be present when this drug is dispensed
paedophile	man sexually attracted to children
panic attack	fear, usually onsets without warning
pantomime	Early English comic theatre
paranoia	psychological fear without factual basis
paranoid schizophrenia	form of schizophrenia with an obsession e.g. pursuit by devils
Parkinson's Disease	disease characterised by tremors in the body
Patch Adams, Dr	American psychiatrist who developed humour therapy
patient	term applied to people in a hospital or being seen by therapist
Pavlov, Ivan Petrovich	Neurologist who developed theory of conditioned response
peer	someone of the same level e.g. age group, intellect, interest
pen portrait	or 'vignette' - a written description, which describes a person
persistent ideas / thoughts	unwanted ideas or thoughts which will not go away
persistent images	as above, but visual images
personal resource	an individual's own way of coping with something
personality disorders	mental illness, characterised by problems of the personality
pharmaceutical	relating to the pharmaceutical or drugs industry
pharmaceutical drugs	medications made of synthetic materials or plants in laboratories
Pharmacist	scientist - prescribes drugs [also Apothecary, Chymist, Druggist]
Phineas Gage	A Victorian worker whose damaged skull was examined after his death.

phobia	deep-rooted fear of something specific - e.g. spiders, flying, dirt
phrenology	discredited study of character read from lumps on the head
physiotherapy	a physical therapy, involving massage and manipulation
placebo test	inert medication, given to some patients as part of drug trial tests
Plato	Greek Philosopher interested in the study of the mind
Play Therapy	a therapy used specifically to help children
pleasure-pain principle	Early Freudian theory that man seeks pleasure and avoids pain
POM	prescription only drugs
possessed	belief that evil spirits can 'possess' a living person
post-hypnotic suggestion	suggestion implanted by Hypnotherapist in client's unconscious
post traumatic stress	stress after a traumatic event, e.g. an accident
poverty trap	no free income for training or improving life
pow-wow (or palaver)	tribal meetings; to resolve social problems
Power of Attorney	legal power to direct day-to-day affairs of someone considered unfit to do it themselves
prana	Hindu medicine; the body's lifeforce
preparation	medication or drug; sometimes prepared from basic chemicals
Primary Care Team	G.P.s and the various therapists within G.P. Practices
Pro Life Organisation	student body opposed to euthanasia, assisted suicide & abortion
Project Atlas (WHO)	WHO project; mapping mental health resources world wide

proprietary medication	drugs which are sold 'over the counter' without prescription
psyche	human soul or mind; Psyche was a Greek goddess
psychiatric hospital	hospital for the care of the mentally ill
Psychiatrist	a doctor with an extra qualification in psychiatric medicine
psychiatry	treatment and study of mental disorders
psycho analysis	therapy developed by Sigmund Freud; analysing the mind
Psycho Analyst	therapist; practices psycho-analysis
psycho-dynamic	resolving current problems by understanding past relationships
psycho-educational	psychological training e.g. stress management, assertiveness
psychodrama	therapy involving 'acting out' scenes from the patient's life
'psychological balance'	term - describes mental well being
'psychological cosh'	slang term; tranquillisers used to dampen unwanted behaviours
psychology	the study of human behaviour
psychomotor agitation	state of frantic activity
psychomotor retardation	extreme lethargy, as in clinical depression
psychopath	personality disorder characterised by absence of conscience
psychosis	visual and auditory hallucinations
psychosurgery	brain surgery
Psychotherapist	therapist using talking cure; enabling client to develop insights
Puer Eternis	the eternal youth; a man who acts like an immature youth
purge (verb)	to give an enema; historic cure for all sorts of medical ailments

Q

qi	body's energy [Japanese medicine]
Qi Gong	Chinese exercise and soft martial art

R

refer	to introduce a patient
'regular'	slang term for someone who is regularly in and out of prison
Rehabilitation Officer	therapist enabling mental health clients to live in the community
Rehabilitation Units	cross between a therapeutic community & psychiatric hospital
religious	someone who devotes themselves to a particular set of beliefs
religious images	hallucinations of a religious kind e.g. of the Virgin Mary or God
remedy	cure or therapy; usually applied to holistic medicine
repressed	hidden in the unconscious mind; not consciously aware of
research	systematic study to add to the knowledge of illness and its cure
resilience (in a therapist)	ability to carry out therapy without becoming over-involved
resistance	deliberate or unconscious opposition e.g. of a thought or idea
Responsible Medical Officer	Doctor delegated to oversee patient detained under the Mental Health Act
rite (or ritual)	ceremony to mark the main life changes e.g. birth, middle age
ritual (in illness)	repetition of a certain act which it is believed cures a situation
Royal College of Psychiatrists	UK professional body of Psychiatrists

S

Samaritans	organisation started by Chad Varah to help suicidal people
sanctuary	similar to asylum; a place of peace where someone feels secure
Sane (organisation)	a mental health charity

274

sanity	sound mind; able to distinguish between real & imagined events
scapegoat	sacrificed animal or person, who represents sins of community
'schizo'	derogatory term - someone with schizophrenia / mental illness
schizoid	personality disorder characterised by detachment from society
schizophrenia	mental illness with symptoms of delusions & hallucinations
School of Thought	a particular method of training; taught by an individual school
'screws'	prison officers (slang term commonly used by prisoners)
'script'	slang term for prescription
'section' / 'sectioning'	slang term meaning detained under the Mental Health Act
sedative	drug to calm nervous system
self hypnosis	voluntary state of deep relaxation - enables the unconscious mind
self understanding	process by which patients/clients learn about their characteristics
Seeker	one who seeks knowledge, particularly from seers or prophets
serotonin	chemical transmitter in the brain (see also noradrenaline)
session	an amount of therapeutic time, usually 45 minutes to 1 hour
Shadow	Jungian archetype; the part of ourselves which is evil
'shaking palsy'	historic term for epilepsy or a form of Parkinson's Disease
shiatsu	Japanese massage using the fingertips on pressure points
Skinner, Burrus Frederic	Scientist - developed behavioural theory from Thorndike's theory
side effect	the unwanted effects of drugs (see also 'negative effect')

social housing	housing provided at low cost by Local Authorities
social integration	being a part of society
'social misfit'	historic term for anyone outside society; prostitute, tramp, thief
social phobia	fear of social situations
social rules	unwritten rules which are observed in human communities
Social Worker	therapist who helps to resolve social orientated problems
solitary confinement	form of punishment in prison; person is detained in isolation
solution-focused therapy	brief therapy; helps patients find solutions to life problems
Spanish Inquisition	Medieval men delegated by the Pope to try and sentence witches
'speaking in tongues'	'babbling'-like speech; accepted in some sects as 'voices of God'
spiritual	accepting there is more than body and mind; morality & values
Spiritualists	religious sect who use Mediums to talk with the dead
split personality disorder	markedly different personality characteristics within a person
SSRI's	Specific Serotonin Re-Uptake Inhibitor; antidepressants
stigma	a negative opinion fuelled by lack of knowledge
stimulant	drug or remedy which revives or increases energy
strait jacket	historic canvas jacket binding a patient's arms to prevent violence
stress	the forces which determine action
stupefaction	lethargic and immobile state (as in severe depression)
sub personality	an individual characteristic of a person (see archetype)
subconscious	level through which material passes to the conscious mind

suicidal	clinical term; considering suicide
suicide	deliberately taking one's own life
Suicide Act 1961	Act under which it is illegal to assist someone to commit suicide
'suicide tourism'	new term; those who go abroad to commit suicide using the facilities of clinics or organisations set up to assist with this act
supermodels	one of the few fashion models who are regularly in the media
Supervisor (therapy)	person a therapist sees to discuss and overview patients
supervision	learning through discussing patients with an experienced therapist
symptom	a sign, usually of an illness
synthesised/ synthesis	combining individual chemicals for example to make new drugs

T

Tai Chi	Chinese exercise and soft martial art
talking cure	therapies use talking to effect a cure
tangible	physically real
Taoism	sect of Buddhism - 'The Way'
tardive dyskinesia	tongue rolling, grimacing, through long term use of medication
The Mental Health Act	in the UK, the Act concerned with care of the mentally ill
'The Scream'	famous painting by Mung; agonised ghost-like face, screaming
Therapeutic Community	a community of mentally ill residents and their therapists
'therapeutic hour'	30 minutes to 45 minutes
Therapist	one who cures by using a therapy
therapy	cure for physical or mental illness; not necessarily medical
Thorndike, Edward	Behaviourist who worked on reward & behaviour responses

tic	spasm of muscles causing involuntary movement e.g. on the face
Together	Mental health aftercare charity (formerly known as Maca)
tools [in therapy]	methods used by Therapist
'top [myself]'	slang term - to commit suicide
'topping and tailing'	slang term used in clinics and hospitals for bathing patients
Tourettes Syndrome	condition with facial & body twitches of an intolerable nature
toxic psychosis	caused by prescribing poor drug combinations, or drug abuse
toxicity	level of toxin or poison
tramp	literally someone who tramps the streets; is homeless
trance	deep relaxation; the unconscious mind is open to suggestion
tranquilliser or 'tranny'	drug which suppresses or calms part of the nervous system
trauma	shock
trepanning	cutting a small circle out of the skull; primitive psycho-surgery
Tribunal [mental health]	committee of professionals and lay people
tricyclic	type of antidepressant; chemical structure has 3 ('tri') rings
'trip'	hallucination induced by illegal drugs or part of psychotic illness
twitch	slang word see 'tic'; symptom of Tourettes Disorder

U

unconscious	part of the mind hidden from awareness
uncovered	term used in therapy to describe when something is realized

V

valium	addictive tranquilliser once widely prescribed to women

virtual drug trial	testing new drugs using specialised computer programmes
virtual modelling	see 'computer modelling'
visualisation	imagining an event with the purpose of helping it become real
vital fluids	see 'humour'
voodoo and witchcraft	a cult practised in Haiti

W

warrant	a legal document, usually for arrest or entry to private dwelling
Watson , John Broadus	Psychologist who developed the learned behavioural theory
White Paper	proposals from the Government for new pieces of legislation
Wise Old Man (Woman)	Jungian archetype; part of ourselves which shows wisdom
Witch	ancient term; a human servant of the devil, either male or female
witchcraft	the practice of magic, for good or evil purposes
'witch hunt'	literally a search for witches; now means 'finding a scapegoat'
'witch mark'	historic term for a nipple (fatty growth) where imps suckled
'word salad'	babbling, as in forms of schizophrenia
World Health Organisation (WHO)	a consortium of many countries who come together to improve standards in health care & carry out research into better health
WRVS	Women's Royal Voluntary Service; provide hospital comforts

Y

yin and yang	two opposing forces in the body [Chinese medicine]
Yoga	an Eastern form of physical and spiritual exercise using postures
Yogi	person who practices yoga

Index